CRISTA

20 Wa
Shipston C...

C000127710

Compiled by Peter Titchmarsh, in memory of his wife, Janet, and with gratitude to the
staff of Shipston Home Nursing and Shipston's Community Nurses

CONTENTS

INTRODUCTORY SECTION

Published by:
The Macmillan Way Association
on behalf of:
Shipston Home Nursing,
Lower Farm Barn,
Great Wolford,
CV36 5NQ

© Shipston Home Nursing 2018

First published
1st February 2013
Fourth Edition
ISBN 0-9526851-7-5

Front Cover Photograph:
Shipston Country from
Sunrising Hill
(*see page 91*)

Introducing Shipston Country

Perhaps you have not heard the name Shipston Country before? However the area in which Shipston lies is so attractive that you are certain to hear it often mentioned in the future. If this guidebook is judged to be partially responsible, the author makes no apology. But he should at least explain himself.

What is Shipston Country? It is centred upon the attractive little market town of Shipston-on-Stour. This is itself situated about midway between the source of the Stour in the hills above the Sibfords and its confluence with the Avon below Stratford-upon-Avon. This delightful little river is the principal feature of Shipston Country's northern half, while the southern half, along with much of its western fringes, merges into Cotswold country. Many of the villages to the east of the Stour valley lie in low, rolling country which runs towards the northern edge of the beautiful, but under-rated Oxfordshire Cotswolds, parts of which also lie within Shipston Country. To the west are the northern ramparts of the classic Cotswolds, amongst which are several Shipston Country villages.

On pages 5-52 we provide details of twenty walks in ascending order of length, from under two miles to ten miles. On pages 53-96 Shipston Country's towns, villages and other places of interest are described. While this guidebook's main objective is to offer a series of entertaining walks together with detailed information on Shipston Country, it is also hoped to help raise funds for Shipston Home Nursing (Registered Charity No. 1162586), whose vitally important work is funded almost entirely by charitable donations. We shall do this by encouraging walkers to raise funds by obtaining sponsorship from friends, relatives and work colleagues, and we shall also pass all proceeds on the sale of this guidebook to the same organisation.

Our Walks Explained

We suggest that you start your walks early in the day and return to the starting inn for lunch. In every case you should obtain the permission of the inn's management to park your car and if you are returning for lunch this will normally be obtained. If you are unable to obtain permission we can only suggest that you park at the nearest possible alternative.

Each paragraph of text starts with a reference letter and this cross-refers with the same letter on the accompanying maps. These maps are at a scale of 1:50,000 (about one-and-a-quarter inches to the mile) and are based upon the Ordnance Survey's Landranger series. The sheet numbers of the Ordnance Survey's Landranger and Explorer maps covering the area similar to that covered by each of our own maps are also indicated. The symbols and signs used on the maps are shown in the block at the head of page 4 and there is a chart below it showing the OS maps covering the whole area. If a description of any place passed on the walks is included in the Gazetteer Section it will be printed in bold.

Shipston Home Nursing was founded in 1997 by Charlie Wells, a local District Nurse, whose sister Penny Birtwell died of breast cancer in 1992. Penny was young, had a husband with two young children. During her last weeks she remained at home, being looked after by her family and friends. Witnessing Penny's death was deeply painful for all, but gave Charlie a chance to see the enormous value of caring for someone terminally ill in their own home, being looked after by nurses qualified in palliative care and surrounded by their loved ones. From this experience, Charlie realised the enormous need for a "Hospice at Home" service to cover our local community.

So Charlie moved forward, and with the help of local doctors from the Medical Centre at Shipston and local businessmen and friends, Shipston Home Nursing was established. The charity is led by a Board of Trustees, an Executive Director who is responsible for the oversight and coordination of Nursing, Fundraising, Financial and Operational activities and liaising with regulatory bodies and community groups. Our nursing services and the care we provide for the families of our patients is free of charge to anybody that needs our help and our area of benefit includes Shipston, Kineton, Wellesbourne and the surrounding villages. Thank you so much for supporting our charity, your contribution and that of others allows us to continue to support patients and their families during the most difficult of times.

We are always looking for like - minded people who have the necessary skills and enthusiasm to help us to continuously improve the services we offer, if you would like any further information about us please visit www.shipstonhomenursing.co.uk or call us on 01608 664850.

The Countryside Code

Be safe: **Plan Ahead** and follow signs. Be prepared for the unexpected. Please respect the working life of the countryside, as our actions can affect people's livelihoods, our heritage, and the safety and welfare of animals and ourselves. Keep to public paths across farmland and walk in single file to minimise path-spread or crop damage. Use gates and stiles to cross fences, hedges and walls. **Leave gates and property as you find them**. **Take your litter home** . Don't forget that litter is not only untidy, but it can also cause great harm to animals and farm machinery. Make sure you don't harm animals, birds, plants or trees. **Keep dogs under close control,** *keeping them on leads when there is any chance of encountering stock. Don't forget that pregnant ewes are very much at risk even from merely playful dogs.* It is your duty to ensure that your dog is not a danger or a nuisance to farm animals, wildlife or other people. Take special care on country roads, *usually walk towards oncoming traffic, but on blind bends walk on the outside of the bend where you will be most visible.* Make no unnecessary noise. Show consideration for other people and help to make the countryside a pleasant place for all, at home, at work or at leisure.

SYMBOLS, ETC. USED ON WALK MAPS

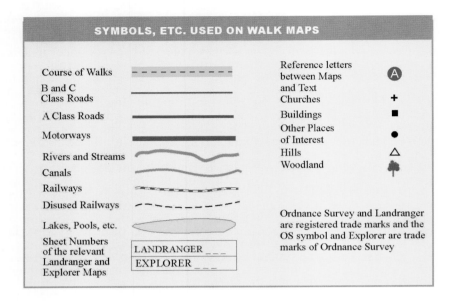

Course of Walks	
B and C Class Roads	
A Class Roads	
Motorways	
Rivers and Streams	
Canals	
Railways	
Disused Railways	
Lakes, Pools, etc.	
Sheet Numbers of the relevant Landranger and Explorer Maps	LANDRANGER _ _ _ EXPLORER _ _ _

Reference letters between Maps and Text   Ⓐ

Churches   +

Buildings   ■

Other Places of Interest   ●

Hills   △

Woodland   🌳

Ordnance Survey and Landranger are registered trade marks and the OS symbol and Explorer are trade marks of Ordnance Survey

ORDNANCE SURVEY MAP COVERAGE OF SHIPSTON COUNTRY

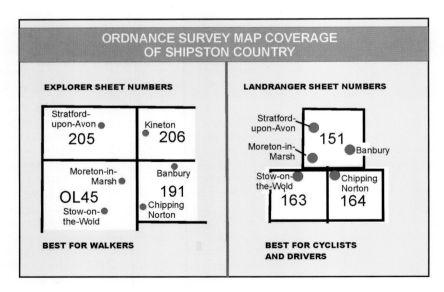

EXPLORER SHEET NUMBERS

Stratford-upon-Avon ●
205

Kineton ● **206**

Moreton-in-Marsh ●
OL45
Stow-on- ●
the-Wold

Banbury
191
● Chipping
Norton

BEST FOR WALKERS

LANDRANGER SHEET NUMBERS

Stratford-upon-Avon
Moreton-in-Marsh
151
● Banbury

Stow-on-the-Wold ●
163

● Chipping Norton
164

BEST FOR CYCLISTS AND DRIVERS

WALK 1
EDGEHILL-RADWAY-EDGEHILL

Start from - The Castle Inn,
Edgehill,
OX15 6DJ
Tel 01295 670 255
Length of walk: 1¼ miles
Approximate time ¾ hour

(A) Set out from the Castle Inn, **Edgehill**, by facing out of its front door and turning left to go under high wooden walkway between the inn's tower and a subsidiary building. Almost immediately go through gateway and turn left at a small crossing of paths. Go down partly-surfaced path with low concrete and steel fence on its right. At end of fence go over another crossing of paths and go through wooden kissing gate into top of large steeply-sloping field, which still shows signs of its parkland origins. The splendid open views ahead must have been all too familiar to the Royalist troops on the eve of the Battle of Edgehill. Go down field with hedge over to right, aiming for gap in cross-hedge below. Through wooden kissing gate in this gap and keep along left-hand edge of next field with fence to immediate left. Radway Grange visible over to right. Through wooden kissing gate at end of field and after a few paces through gateway ahead and keep in same direction onto track.

(B) Pass houses on left at entry to **Radway** village and bear right on surfaced public road by pond on right. Now go onto path on right-hand side of road. Extensive gardens of Radway Grange beyond hedge on right. Bear right, keeping on path to right of road junction (but turn left here if you wish to visit church, which is visible from here). Keep on path passing entrance to Radway Grange on right. Radway's pleasant street has mown grass verges shaded by young trees. Pass *sign - The Green* on the left. Pass Village Hall on left and bus shelter on right and keep on path by adjoining road junction.

[map]
WALK 1   LANDRANGER 151 / EXPLORER 206
RADWAY   Jacob's Ladder
Radway Grange
The Castle Inn **A**
Obelisk
EDGEHILL
© Crown Copyright
0   1/4   1/2
Scale Half-a-mile

(C) At about 70 paces beyond bus shelter turn right up second roadway to right signed *Norton's Lane*. Pass Dugdale House on left and at end of roadway keep in same direction onto public footpath with productive vegetable garden to left. Pass small wooden benches to right and immediately go through wooden kissing gate onto path with fence to left and woodland to right. Soon through another wooden kissing gate into large field, with fence initially still to left. Keep up this large, ever-steepening field heading for woods above and beyond.

(D) Draw breath at top of field and possibly sit on adjoining stone bench before going through wooden kissing gate. Bear right on path into lovely beech woodlands. Now on the course of the **Macmillan Way**. After a few minutes ignore small wooden gate on right, leading into parkland. Pleasant views of parkland to right as our path is on

right-hand edge of wood. Fork left up narrow, possibly overgrown path following Macmillan Way waymark. At this point there is an obelisk in a clump of trees down to right, but this is difficult to spot, especially in summer. Go carefully up slippery and unevenly surfaced path, emerging at top to go over small crossing of paths. Now go through gateway and below high wooden walkway to return to the front door of the Castle Inn, **Edgehill**, thus completing Walk 1 **(A)**.

The Castle Inn, Edgehill

5

WALK 2

ILMINGTON - PIG LANE - LARKSTOKE - ILMINGTON

(A) Set out from the Howard Arms, **Ilmington**, turning right, out of its car park. Go along pavement on right-hand side of quiet road passing attractive cottages on right. Go onto path that extends beyond road's end and climb gently with small stream below to right.

Start from - The Howard Arms,
Ilmington,
CV36 4LT
Tel 01608 682 226
Length of walk: 3 miles
Approximate time: 1½ hours

(B) Turn left onto narrow roadway by small triangular tarmac parking space and soon turn right at T-junction and go along pavement beside wider road known as Front Street (The Red Lion Inn visible back down to left (*Tel: 01608 682 366 Post Code CV36 4LX*). Soon fork left to follow road up across attractive sloping green passing St Philip's Roman Catholic Church up to left. Keep straight along road to go into Grump Street ignoring turn down to right. Pass Raven's Croft (house) on right at end of village and end of road and onto rough track. After about 50 paces turn right through metal kissing gate and veer left to go down field into valley bottom. Go through possibly partly-hidden metal kissing gate below trees, cross small bridge over small stream and through second gate just beyond. Now turn left to go up right-hand side of valley bottom with line of trees to immediate left. Soon starting to climb a little more steeply. Through small metal gate and keep on up next field with trees still to left. Good views opening up behind us. Through gap in sporadic line of scrubby bushes and trees. Still climbing steeply. Through large metal gate and keep up left-hand side of next field.

(C) At top of hill turn right onto well-defined track known as Pig Lane, but not indicated here. Splendid views of the Midland Plain over to right of track. Climb steadily up Pig Lane, partly overhung by trees for short distance. Radio masts soon visible ahead. Through small wooden gate beside large metal one with radio masts on immediate left. Follow Pig Lane into narrow belt of woodland, drop down to cross wider area and then veer slightly left **to cross public road with great care**. On far side of road go

Above Ilmington, before reaching Pig Lane

through small wooden gate and go up right-hand edge of field with hedge and tree line to immediate right. Soon ignore waymarked path to right and head for small metal gate at top of field. Through this gate and go up steep incline in small wood then bearing right to go onto long path between hedges.

(D) Through small wooden gate beside large one and turn right on to narrow public road with the Larkstoke Television Transmitter just beyond road. Go down along narrow, normally quiet road ignoring bridleway sign to right close to series of large stones lining unusually wide grass verge. Road starts to descend more steeply and also bends to right. Go further down road taking in the splendid views down ahead but making sure not to miss gap on right with possibly partly-concealed waymark on post.

(E) Turn right through this large gap, leaving narrow road and going straight across field. At end of field go through gap and keep in same direction down through young plantation. Go into much more mature wood veering very slightly right. On meeting large wooden gate ahead turn left to go down slope which could be very slippery after rain. On emerging from wood through small wooden gate, keep in same direction to go straight down field (B&B signed up to left at this point). Drop down

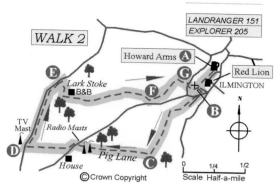

into wooded valley bottom, no sign of stream in summer. Immediately beyond valley bottom veer left following direction of waymark on post to go up bank. Soon turn left to go over bridge and through small wooden gate. Keep in same direction up bank heading just to right of lone tree on skyline and soon pass confirming waymark post. Continue across field passing second waymark post. Through large metal gate in tree-lined cross-hedge and follow track just to left of fenceline. Fine open views over to left. At top, right-hand corner of field go through large metal gate into woodlands following tree-shaded track. Go under low-voltage power-line and follow track as it bends to right.

(F) Through large metal gate keeping on track and just before reaching public road, bear left to go over stile. Now veer left along top of field with hedge on immediate left. Veer left to go through wooden kissing gate entering a permissive area ("part of a wider environmental scheme"). Keep along left-hand edge of field as it bears down to right. At bottom left-hand edge of field go over stile and immediately turn right following waymark direction. Keep down narrow, grassy strip which we follow as it bends to right before going over 2nd stile this one being beside large metal gate. Keep on track as it drops down into outskirts of **Ilmington**. Just before reaching first house on right, turn left to go through waymarked wooden gate, and veer left across small stable yard. Turn right immediately beyond wooden stables on right and down narrow, partly-stepped path.

(G) Go over public road **with great care** and turn right along its left-hand side, with churchyard on left. Turn left to go down path with churchyard on immediate left and high stone wall to right. Pass entrance to church's south doorway down to left (*church well worth visiting*). Turn left at corner of churchyard and turn right by Church Cottage on right. Pass old wellhead in wall to right and ---

Springtime at Ilmington

(B) --- Turn left by small triangular tarmac parking space re-joining outward route. Go down path with small stream below to left. Pass cottages on left and soon turn left into the Howard Arms car park, thus completing Walk 2 **(A)**.

.

WALK 3

PAXFORD - EBRINGTON - PAXFORD

(A) Set out from the Churchill Arms, **Paxford**. With your back to its front door turn right and immediately cross road **with care** at T-junction and go through wooden kissing gate well to the right of the church. Go down right-hand side of field with hedge over to right. Near bottom of field veer slightly left to go over wooden bridge crossing stream. Turn right beyond bridge and walk parallel with stream on right. At end of field go over stile and keep straight ahead into

Start from - The Churchill Arms, Paxford, GL55 6XH Tel 01386 593 159 Length of walk: 3 miles Approximate time: 1½ hours

plantation going along grassy path as close as possible to the bank of stream on right and ignoring any possible paths to left. At end of plantation go through wooden kissing gate and turn right with care to go beside public road. Over slight bridge crossing stream and immediately turn left to go over stile. Cross narrow field and go through small wooden gate into possibly overgrown plantation. If too overgrown veer right with care up bank and bear left at top to go along left-hand edge of field. Eventually cross surfaced track with bridge to immediate left and continue along left-hand edge of field. At end of field go through small wooden gate, cross possible horse-gallop and through second small wooden gate to keep along left-hand edge of next field. As field edge curves to right with thick bushes to left **start to look with care** for waymark on small post on left indicating path going down left, into woodland. Go down bank on this path into woodland and turn left to go over small wooden bridge. Veer right beyond bridge to go parallel with stream and then ---

(B) --- turn right onto public road, known here as Pudlicott Lane, **with very great care** and almost immediately turn left, off road and go over small bridge. Go up steps into woodland with house visible over to left and attractive pool to right, which was once the mill pond for Pudlicott Mill. Through wooden kissing gate and veer slightly right to cross mown area with garden to left. Over stile to right of large wooden gate and turn right to go on farm track along right-hand edge of field with wooded area to right.

The Churchill Arms, Paxford

Ebrington visible ahead left. At end of track turn left **with care** to go beside public road. Road soon starts to climb gently. Pass modern Cotswold stone farmhouse on left. Ebrington entry signed.

(C) Ignore paths to left and right, although we shall come back to this point later. Arrive at the centre of **Ebrington** with small triangular, tree-shaded green complete with interesting Millennium Mosaic. Metal seats encircling the trees provide a good resting opportunity.

(D) Bear right by the Ebrington Arms (*Tel: 01386 593 223 - Post Code GL55 6NH*) on right and the village green, now on left. Pass phone box on right and soon turn right, down cul-de-sac road (sign - *Coldicott Leys*). At end of road go through wooden kissing gate and over stile just beyond. Turn right beyond stile and soon go onto track across top of field. Go over stile to right of large metal gate. Keep straight along track with fence to right and farm buildings over to left.

(C1) At end of track go through large metal gate and turn left **with care** onto public road, which we used for our entry to Ebrington. After 50 paces turn left, off road, and go down left-hand edge of sloping field. About halfway down field watch carefully for stile in hedge on left. Turn left over this stile and veer right to go down field aiming for right-hand willow tree in cross-hedge below. Go over small wooden bridge below willow trees and keep in same direction across next field to go over two rudimentary stiles in cross-fences. Hedge now on left and in left-hand corner of field go through large metal gate. Go over bridge and bear right following waymark direction to cross corner of field aiming for gap in cross-hedge. Through squeeze-stile in gap and over small bridge. Veer left aiming for gateway in far corner of field following waymark direction.

WALK 3

© Crown Copyright

LANDRANGER 151
EXPLORER OL45

Scale Half-a-mile

(E) Through large metal gate in corner of field and turn left **with great care** to go on opposite verge beside very busy minor road . After 50 paces turn right to go onto surfaced drive and over stile beside large wooden gate. Go up well-surfaced, tree-lined drive leading to Marfurlong Farm. At end of hedge on left turn right, off drive and go diagonally, up across field aiming for wooden kissing gate in wooden fence. Go through this kissing gate and veer slightly right across corner of field. Through wooden kissing gate in wooden fence, over small bridge and go straight across next field aiming for

Houses beside the churchyard, Ebrington

gap in cross-hedge ahead. Fine views back to **Ebrington**. Through this gap in cross-hedge and veer slightly right to cross very large, undulating field, aiming, when it becomes visible, just to right of dilapidated wind pump with tank on tall metal supports. Beyond windpump aim just to right of conifer trees with farm buildings behind them.

(F) Go through gap to immediate right of conifer trees with small greenhouse just ahead and farm building to left, and immediately turn right to go down grassy path with wooden fence to right. Attractive pool soon visible down to left. At end of fence turn left in corner to keep on grassy path with hedge now on right. Turn right **with care** on to public road and immediately keep straight, not right at road T-junction (sign - *Paxford*). Pass **Paxford** entry sign and follow road through village, first turning left beyond 30 mph sign (sign - *Blockley*). Keep along footpath on right-hand side of road. Bear right by triangular green (sign - *Blockley*) and on reaching Churchill Arms on left, cross road to it **with care**, thus completing Walk 3 **(A)**.

9

WALK 4

EBRINGTON - FOXCOTE - EBRINGTON

Start from - The Ebrington Arms,
Ebrington,
GL55 6NH
Tel 01386 593 223
Length of walk: 3¼ miles
Approximate time: 1¾ hours

(A) Set out from the Ebrington Arms, **Ebrington**, crossing small triangular green beneath oak trees sheltering the interesting Millennium Mosaic Sundial (*use your walking stick as a temporary gnomon!*). Pass War Memorial on left and go along path on left-hand side of road (sign - *Mickleton*), soon passing path to left leading to church. Almost immediately bear right to cross road to path on right-hand side of road passing attractive cottages, many of which are thatched. Go straight ahead at road junction (sign - *The Hidcotes*) and soon, just beyond Village Hall on left, turn right to go over old stone stile (sign - *Public footpath*) and then over wooden stile. Bear left across grassy space and do not go straight ahead, but go over left-hand wooden stile beside large metal gate. Go along right-hand edge of field with wooden fence to right. At end of field go over wooden stile beneath bushes and, then ignoring small wooden bridge to sharp left, bear left into field. Go up left-hand edge of field with hedge to immediate left. At end of field go over waymarked wooden bridge crossing wide ditch. Go up left-hand edge of next field with tree-sheltered hedge to immediate left. Now climbing steadily.

(B) Turn right at top of field and after about 30 paces, turn left to go over wooden stile. Veer very slightly right to go up across field. Over stile and veer slightly right to go across next field - path starting to level out. Fine southward views opening out behind us. Over stile and keep in same direction across next field - a relief to be at the top of our climb. At end of field go through wide gap and veer slightly right to go along grassy track with hedge to left and fence to right - an attractive terrace walk with splendid views to right. Ebrington Hill Farm's buildings visible ahead right. Turn right to go through small wooden gate into wooded area, immediately bearing left, thus keeping in same direction as track, now parallel to our left. Follow path as it eventually meanders to right and drops steeply down to farm drive. Now turn left to follow still-wooded drive until it bends up to left and at this point turn right onto path. Watch for this with care - waymark post may be obscured by vegetation. Soon emerge from wooded area into field and keep along right-hand edge of field with bushy hedge to immediate right.

The War Memorial, Ebrington

(C) Turn right where hedge turns right following waymark and still keeping hedge to immediate right. At end of field go through very large gap and keep along right-hand edge of next field immediately going below large ash tree. At end of field keep in same direction to go over x-rds of tracks below another large ash tree and ignoring gate to right. Go along track with

10

woodland on left but when track starts to bend to left, go straight ahead for about 12 paces and then turn right, down a defined path below trees. Go through waymarked gap into more open area with views opening out ahead and two radio masts visible over to left. Go down path with fence to left and walls to right. Foxcote Farm farmhouse visible in valley ahead left. Now start to drop down into valley on possibly overgrown path. Through small wooden gate and veer left down across field aiming for small gate near left-hand end of cross-fence below. Modern farm buildings at right-hand end of fence. Go through small wooden gate in cross-fence and turn left onto well-surfaced estate road immediately passing Foxcote Farmhouse on left. Keep on estate road down into valley passing a house on right. Soon start to climb out of valley with mown

WALK 4

© Crown Copyright

LANDRANGER 151
EXPLORER OL45

grass verges and a high Leylandii hedge to right, which provides privacy for the mansion and garden of Foxcote House. Through small metal gate beside cattle-grid. Keep on estate road as it veers to right at junction of estate roads and pass gated entrance to Foxcote House on right (*please do not linger or intrude upon the privacy of the occupants*). Veer to left by cattle-grid over to right and go down into valley on rougher track. Just beyond valley bottom go through small wooden gate beside cattle-grid and climb up track beyond.

(D) After about 40 paces turn right to go on meandering path through dark conifer wood (*keep dogs on lead - this is a shooting estate*). Emerge from wood and keep in same direction across narrow field to go through gap in cross-hedge with possible large wooden gate. Keep in same direction across next sloping field soon running parallel with woods not far down to right and gradually getting closer to them. At end of field join track and follow it, keeping in same direction. Keep on track as it gently rises and then starts to drop down with barn soon visible ahead. Ignore track down to right where woodlands on right end. Ignore grassy track up to left at start of woodlands on left. Keep on track as it veers to left on meeting large stone barn (Hoarston). Keep on track as it starts to drop down beyond barn, but at waymark post on left (with fore and aft waymarks, but without waymark in our required direction), turn right, off track and go down across field heading for its low corner.

(E) In low corner of field go over small waymarked bridge beneath willow tree and immediately turn left. Now go along field with trees and hedge to left but soon turn right onto track going up across field. Near top of rise turn left immediately beyond small, largely-concealed building to go through gap below ash tree. Follow track along left-hand edge of field and at end of hedge on left and just before meeting low-voltage power-line, turn right up track, going parallel with power-line now to left. Go over wooden stile to right of large metal gate and initially keep in same direction. But soon veer left to go up partially-surfaced driveway. At top of slope veer left onto better-surfaced roadway, soon passing wood to left and tall hedge to right. Emerge into more open area with a group of modern houses down to left. Soon veer right onto public road **with great care** at entry to **Ebrington**. Walk carefully along right-hand side of road and soon go onto footpath on right-hand side of road. Near top of rise turn left by small green and return to the Ebrington Arms, thus completing Walk 4 **(A)**.

WALK 5

COMBROOK - COMPTON VERNEY - COMBROOK

--- *A Capability Brown Landscape*

(A) Set out from **Combrook** Church, going along minor road between church on right and Village Hall on left. Ignore path up to right just before elaborate Victorian horse-drinking trough on right.

Start from - Combrook Church, CV35 9HN
Length of walk: 3½ miles
Approximate time: 2 hours

After about 35 paces beyond trough, turn left to go down path with hedges on both sides. Through small wooden gate, cross stream and go up bank. Bear right at top of bank and go along wide grassy way with garden hedge to left and post and rail fence to right. Ignore stile on left. Lake now visible to right, although the dam that forms it is not easy to spot. Through small wooden gate ahead and onto gently-descending path in woodland. Attractive views of lake through trees to right. At end of woodland go through small wooden gate into open parkland, once part of the **Compton Verney** estate, with splendid oak trees. This, along with the lake, being the work of 18th-century landscape designer, Capability Brown. Initially go parallel with lake shore but soon veer slightly left to follow waymark direction (on post). At top of slight rise head for distant waymark post on a line just to right of two farm cottages ahead. Through small metal gate to left of large metal gate and go along left-hand edge of next field with post and rail fence to left. At 15 paces beyond transformer on power-pole turn left to go through small metal gate and turn right to continue in same direction along well-surfaced farm drive. Soon ignore drive to right and go well beyond.

(B) At end of drive, turn left **with great care** onto busy B4086 and go up hill on wide, left-hand grass verge. At top of hill cross road **with great care** and go onto drive to immediate right of Compton Verney Lodge. Go through small gate to right of cattle-grid and down very straight surfaced drive. Over x-rds of drives and soon turn right in the vicinity of Home Farm House (bungalow) and farm buildings keeping on surfaced drive. Pass stable yard on left leaving

Lake just beyond Combrook

surfaced drive and go through large metal gate (bridleway signed). Keep on track in same direction with fence to left and open field to right. Through second large metal gate and veer well to left following track across field which soon becomes more pronounced. This field must have been part of the park in days gone by. Restricted views of lake in valley down to right, although these soon become clearer. Look back for distant view of **Compton Verney** mansion and its bridge and conical roofed icehouse. At end of field meet short length of fence on right before going through large metal gate onto well-defined track with fence initially to right and open field to left. Soon open on both sides. Very pleasant open views ahead.

(C) Go to left of large metal gate and turn right **with care** onto public road. Keep along right-hand side to face oncoming traffic. Over bridge crossing the small stream that feeds Compton Verney's lakes, and keep up beside road. Near top of hill and just short of oak tree on right of road, turn right through kissing gate. Go straight across large field planted with young trees protected by guard fencing. Both this and the next field will become part of Compton Verney's restored parkland. Keep along slope well above valley bottom to right and eventually aim for gap in tree-sheltered cross-hedge ahead. Views of mansion ahead right. Through kissing gate beside large wooden gate in this gap. Keep in same direction across this next field aiming for the approximate centre of a line of tall fir trees ahead. Conical roofed icehouse now visible ahead right. At end of field go through kissing gate beneath fir trees and veer slightly left to go along close to the

WALK 5

LANDRANGER 151
EXPLORER 206

edge of **Compton Verney's** visitor car park. Veer slightly right where grassy track veers to left and follow unsigned pathway below trees. Soon arrive at a small waymarked bridge and cross this to emerge near Compton Verney's vehicle entrance.

(**D**) Turn right **with care** to go along grass verge on right-hand side of the busy B4086 immediately passing the original entrance gates to **Compton Verney**. After a further 30 paces turn left to cross road **with great care** and, by bus stop sign, go onto waymarked path and up across field towards wood on skyline. Beyond brow go through waymarked gap into large wood, with path through it soon becoming a grassy track. Go straight, not left twice, at junctions of tracks. Public road, which runs parallel to our track, now momentarily visible over to left. Track soon changes into a narrow path, but still well-defined. At edge of wood go through gap beside waymarked stile and go down field aiming to left of large ash tree and right-hand end

of postwar house in valley - this is on the edge of **Combrook**. Go through small wooden gate to immediate right of house's garden and then turn left onto public road in **Combrook** by Victorian horse-drinking trough along to right, thereby rejoining our outward route. Now retrace your steps to **Combrook** Church, thus completing Walk 5 (**A**).

Beyond Compton Verney, approaching Point C

13

WALK 6

CLIFFORD CHAMBERS - ATHERSTONE-ON-STOUR -

PRESTON-ON-STOUR - CLIFFORD CHAMBERS

(A) Set out from the New Inn, **Clifford Chambers**, and go into the village, keeping to the pavement on the left-hand side of the road. Pass church and War Memorial on left. Before reaching the gates of beautiful Clifford Manor - straight ahead, turn right, off road, onto short driveway of house called *Palings* and then veer straight ahead onto grassy track to immediate right of house. (*We have now joined* **Shakespeare's Way** *which we shall follow as far as Preston-on-Stour.*) Turn left at T-junction of paths in bushy area and go along tree-bordered path.

> Start from - The New Inn,
> Clifford Chambers,
> CV37 8HR
> Tel 01789 293 402
> Length of walk: 4 miles
> Approximate time: 2 hours

(B) Soon go slightly left, to cross farm road onto narrow path with iron fence on right and holly hedge on left. At end of path keep in same direction on grassy track across large open fields (*but first look back, left, to see brick-built gazebo - the work of Sir Edwin Lutyens we presume*). *The dumpy spire of Atherstone-on-Stour Church soon visible ahead.* Through very wide gap in cross-hedge with large metal gates and keep in same direction, now on smooth-surfaced farm track (*caution - this can be very slippery after rain - the compiler came to grief here!*). Pass large barn on right and bear left onto minor public road in minute **Atherstone-on-Stour**. Pass Victorian church on left (*now in private hands*) and pass barns converted into offices, with yard just beyond, both on left.

(C) Where road bends to left to cross River Stour, turn right, off road, onto small tree-sheltered track. *Good views over to left of handsome early-Gothic-Revival mansion,* **Alscot Park**, *around which we are now going to skirt*. Up this short track and along left-hand edge of field. Bear slightly left and then right with woodland now to left. Soon enter woodland to go along path just inside it with its edge visible to right. Turn left at top corner of wood and keep along left-hand edge of field, with wood still to immediate left. At end of wood go through wooden kissing gate on left. *Mound to our immediate left is all that remains of an old summerhouse's foundations!* Bear right to follow well-used path across undulating field aiming for V in outline of woods ahead. Good views over

Tree-shaded green at Clifford Chambers

to left of **Alscot Park** and the meandering River Stour.

(D) At end of field, go through wooden kissing gate and bear right up pathway through scrubby little wood with nettles, soon joining end of surfaced public road at entry to **Preston-on-Stour**. Pass *The Old Vicarage* on left and soon turn right to follow path up right-hand edge of attractive village green overlooked by timbered and mellow-brick houses, with

14

low garden wall to immediate right. Cross roadway and go through handsome wrought-iron gates into churchyard. Go up yew-shaded path and skirt around the right-hand side of the church. Go out of churchyard through gate opposite west door of church. Now turn right, *leaving Shakespeare's Way*, and go along grassy track beneath trees. Turn left onto minor public road by gate with lodge, leaving Preston-on-Stour. Go up road passing large wood on right. *Good views opening up over to left - both Brailes Hill and Ilmington Hill clearly visible.* Bend sharply to right at top of rise - wood still on right. *Good views of the Cotswold Edge now over to left.* Still on public road, start to drop down a little and beyond end of wood pass driveway to Atherstone Hill (farmhouse) on right. Follow road as it bends to right and then to left. Large wood now on left.

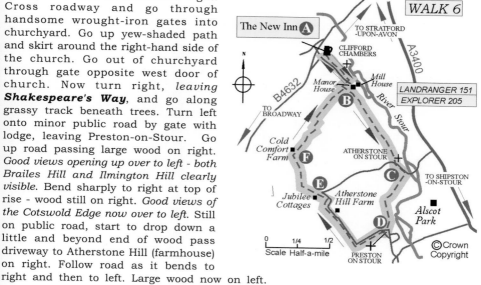

(E) Turn left at T-junction onto unsurfaced track by Jubilee Cottages on left (not indicated) and then turn right onto unsurfaced track (*modestly signed as Cycleway S1*). Start to drop down and at end of wood on right, turn right to go over waymarked stile. Go straight across field on hopefully well-marked path. At far side of field go over stile in thick hedge and keep in same direction across young plantation. Ensure all dogs are on leads as it is now necessary to cross training gallop with great care. Keep in same direction along pathway between hedges.

At Preston-on-Stour

(F) Just before reaching Cold Comfort Farm (not indicated) ahead left, turn right through small metal gate (possibly not waymarked) and go up left-hand side of large field. Hedge on left becomes more sporadic, allowing view of gallop to left. Good views ahead as we top the rise, hedge now on left again as we start to drop gently down. Through waymarked gap at end of field and keep in same direction with wood now on left. Turn left at corner of wood, then turn right at corner of field and keep along its left-hand edge, going down with hedge on immediate left. At bottom of field turn right onto track and almost immediately fork left and bear left, with farm buildings on right. Go down farm track and ---

(B1) ---after passing another farmyard on right, turn left off track onto pathway through bushes (waymarked **Shakespeare's Way**) (this is common with Point **B**, as we are now going to retrace our steps into Clifford Chambers). After 45 paces turn right onto pathway initially in bushes. At end of pathway, turn left onto road in **Clifford Chambers**. Use pavement on far side of road - pass church on right and walk through village eventually arriving back at the New Inn, thus completing Walk 6 **(A)**.

15

WALK 7

BLOCKLEY - BATSFORD - BLOCKLEY

(A) Set out from the Great Western Arms, **Blockley** by turning left out of its car park to go beside public road **with great care**. Almost immediately go over x-rds to go down Lower Street. Turn left immediately beyond Lower Brook House, which is on left, to go up minor road (sign - *Pasture Farm*). Keep out of **Blockley** on road which soon becomes farm track with

Start from - The Great Western Arms, Blockley, GL56 9DT
Tel: 01386 700 362
Length of walk: 4½ miles
Approximate time: 2¼ hours

good views back to village as we climb up track. Where track bends to left, go straight ahead off track to walk to immediate right of barn following bridleway waymark. Keep up right-hand edge of field with hedge to immediate right. Through small wooden gate and keep up path with bushes on both sides. Follow path as it bends to left with low-voltage power-line running parallel to our left and trees and low stone wall to right. At end of stone wall on right go through small wooden gate and keep in almost the same direction across small, scrubby area. Emerge into field and follow along its left-hand edge with hedge to immediate left. Through small wooden gate and keep along left-hand edge for about 50 paces before bearing right to cross field diagonally aiming for gateway in corner following waymark's direction.

(B) In corner of field go through metal gate and keep straight ahead with care onto public road at its corner. (*We shall now have to keep on road for about half a mile.*) (*To make a much shorter walk, turn right here and walk along road **with care** until reaching wood on left-hand side, where you will link with Point E by turning right to go through right-hand of two gates and following our route back to Blockley.*) For main route go straight ahead, down road and eventually pass small stone house on left as we start to drop more steeply down. Pass farm buildings and stables on right. Go straight over x-rds **with care** (*But turn right if you wish to visit **Batsford** Church*).

(C) Over diagonal x-rds **with care** and after about 100 paces turn right, off road and go through small wooden gate (sign - *Public Footpath*). Go along pleasant grassy path overhung by trees. Veer left through narrow gateway and keep in same direction along field edge with hedge and trees to immediate right. Veer left at end of field and almost immediately turn right to go over stile to right of large metal gate. Keep in same general direction following waymark's direction and head

Blockley

towards large wooden gate. Through this gate and keep in same direction along right-hand edge of next field. Through large gap into next field keeping in same direction with wall to immediate right. Through large wooden gate and immediately turn right to go up right-hand edge of field (*if you wish to walk to Moreton-in-Marsh, turn left and link onto Walk 18, just beyond Point F*). Near end of field veer left passing to immediate left of stone house.

(D) Through small wooden gate and, with care, veer right to cross drive leading to **Batsford Arboretum** and go through small wooden gate. (*But walk up drive if you wish to visit Batsford Arboretum.*) (*Now on **The Heart of England Way**, which we shall follow for the rest of our journey back to Blockley.*) Head up across field on well used path and at top of field go over stile to left of large wooden gate. Up grassy bank and veer left onto track overhung by trees. Almost immediately keep right on main track going upwards. Where views open out to left and track veers to left, bear right, off track, to go up

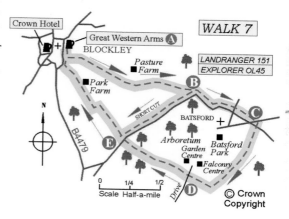

woodland path following waymark's direction. Now climbing steeply with varying woodlands to left and wall to right.

(E) At end of wood go over stile to left of large wooden gate and go straight across road following Heart of England Way waymark. (*We are joined here by the short-cut route from Point B.*) Almost immediately go through right-hand of two gates and go down left-hand side of field with wall to immediate left. At end of field turn left through large wooden gate and follow pathway with bushes on both sides. Turn right to go over stile beside

large metal gate and go steeply down field with hedge and wall over to right, aiming well to left of Park Farm's farmhouse. Good views of Blockley ahead. Over stile to right of large metal gate and follow waymark's direction straight down across field aiming just to left of first power-pole after crossing farm drive. Over stile to left beside large metal gate and go along right-hand edge of field with hedge to immediate right. Over stile beside large metal gate and go down sunken track with trees on both sides. At end of track, turn right **with great care** onto busy public road at our entry to **Blockley**. Soon pass the turn on right to Pasture Farm, which we used near the start of our walk. Pass Lower Brook House on right. Church just visible up to left. Over x-rds bearing right at top of slope (sign - *Northwick Park*) and almost immediately turn right just beyond the Great Western Arms into its car park, thus completing Walk 7 **(A)**.

Batsford Church

17

WALK 8

MICKLETON - KIFTSGATE COURT GARDENS - HIDCOTE GARDENS - LARKSTOKE - HIDCOTE BOYCE - MICKLETON

(A) Set out from the King's Arms Inn, **Mickleton**, crossing the road outside its car park and turning right to go along path beside road, passing Post Office Stores. Where road bends to left, turn right to cross this road **with care** immediately beyond handsome Medford House to go up quieter road. Pass steps up to church on left, veer round to left at effective end of public road and take left-hand fork of footpath signs to go up short roadway.

> Start from - The King's Arms,
> Mickleton,
> GL55 6RT
> Tel 01386 438 257
> Length of walk: 4½ miles
> Approximate time: 2¼ hours

(B) Now go through small wooden gate to immediate left of `new' cemetery. Veer right to cross field aiming for large ash tree in hedgeline (*now following* **The Heart of England Way**). Go through small wooden gate beneath ash tree and go up well-defined path along right-hand edge of field with hedge on immediate right. Keep on path as it veers to right and at end of field go through gateway into next field. Keep along field's right-hand edge with woodlands to right. Leave **The Heart of England Way**, ignoring its sign to right and start to climb gently keeping along field edge. Follow path as it veers to left and soon turn right to go through small wooden gate into rough pasture field. Go straight ahead across sloping field following very slight signs of usage. Veer left going along lower, left-hand slope of valley with woods visible both to right and left, the latter being the outer bounds of Kiftsgate Court Gardens. Keep up valley with field starting to narrow and go through gateway with woods on both sides. Go into next bowl-like field and climb more steeply, aiming for gatepost just visible up ahead. At top of field go right, with lodge beyond wall to left, move a few paces to right to go through wooden gate. Now cross public road with great care and go straight ahead up road signed to Hidcote Gardens NT (*But turn left if you wish to visit* **Kiftsgate Court Gardens**, *the entry to which is only a few yards away*). Continue up road overhung with trees and with glimpses of **Hidcote Gardens** soon evident over to right.

(C) Go straight across **Hidcote Gardens** car park and go up roughly-surfaced roadway (*but turn right if you wish to visit gardens*). Through large metal gate and keep up roadway climbing quite steeply. Splendid views over the Vale of Evesham opening out behind us. Through metal gate where roadway becomes less steep. Keep on main roadway as it turns right and then turns left. Pass **Larkstoke** Television Transmitting Station on left and after going through large metal gate just beyond it ---

(D) -- turn right on to public road. Go along this road until meeting busier road and at this point, turn right to go over stile beside large gate. Go down grassy track initially with fences on both sides, but then stone wall on right. Splendid views ahead. Through metal gate, keep along right-hand edge of field with stone barn well over to left and on reaching bushes veer left to head for waymark post below. This very uneven field is the site of an old quarry. Follow direction of waymark arrow and drop down gradually to large metal gate. Go down large field gradually coming closer to hedgeline on left, with **Hidcote Boyce** soon visible ahead. Where hedgeline turns sharp left, veer left to cut off corner of field and join grassy track near end of field. Go through large metal gate and drop down on track with hedge to right. Through another metal gate and keep on track with field to right and fence to left.

18

(E) Through small wooden gate at entry to **Hidcote Boyce**. Keep straight down road through the delightfully trim hamlet of **Hidcote Boyce** and pass interesting stone sculpture on right just beyond its end. **With great care** go straight over road T-junction just beyond stone sculpture and go through large metal gate. Go down grassy pathway between hedges. Pass young woodland on right and hedge still on left. At end

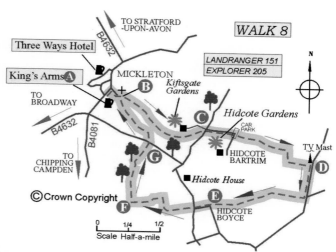

of grassy path go through large metal gate and immediately turn right to go along right-hand edge of field with hedge to immediate right. Turn left in corner of field and go along right-hand edge of field with hedge and trees to immediate right. Veer left at next corner and then start to look carefully for gap in hedge on right. Turn right to go through this gap and over small wooden bridge crossing small stream. Immediately beyond bridge veer slightly right to go up left-hand edge of field with hedge to immediate left.

(F) Near end of field veer left onto track, turn right by small building on left and then turn right again to go along right-hand edge of field with hedge on immediate right, soon going below low-voltage power-line (*now back on **The Heart of England Way***). Good views ahead left. Enter wood and go along path, sometimes narrow and possibly partly overgrown, although some cleared sections reveal fine beech trees. Eventually emerge from wood and follow along left-hand edge of field with wood still to left. Near end of field veer round to right and then turn left to go through small wooden gate. Go down steep, possibly slippery path through woodland and ---

(G) --- go straight across public road **with great care** and through small wooden gate into large sloping field. Mickleton now visible ahead. Go down right-hand side of field aiming for small wooden gate to right of small bushy trees. Through kissing gate leaving **The Heart of England Way** (which goes off to left) and go straight down large field initially keeping some distance away from its right-hand edge. In far right-

Larkstoke near Point D

hand corner of field go through kissing gate into bushy area. Go carefully - path here has tree roots in it and is very uneven. At end of bushy area go through kissing gate into field and keep along its left-hand edge. Mickleton's church spire visible ahead. Pass cemetery wall on right and through wooden kissing gate.

(B) Turn left onto surfaced road at our entry to **Mickleton**, rejoining the outward course of our walk. Pass steps up to church on right. On meeting busier road, cross it with great care and turn left to go along pavement. Pass Post Office Stores on right and then turn left to cross road with great care to arrive back at the car park of the King's Arms, thus completing Walk 8 **(A)**.

19

WALK 9

ODDINGTON - ADLESTROP - DAYLESFORD - ODDINGTON

(A) Set out from the Fox Inn, **Lower Oddington**, by turning left out of its car park and going down left-hand side of minor public road. (*This is on the course of the **Macmillan Way**.*) Turn right at T-junction to go on right-hand side of busy A436 (sign - *Chipping-Norton*). Pass impressive entrance gates on right and keep on verge beside road, but soon cross road **with great care** to use narrow path on left-hand side of road. Over bridge crossing infant River Evenlode and railway line. Site of **Adlestrop's** railway station just along to left.

Start from - The Fox Inn,
Lower Oddington,
GL55 0UR
Tel 01451 870 555
Length of walk: 4¾ miles
Approximate time: 2½ hours

(B) Turn left (with great relief!) off the busy A436 on to minor road (sign - *Adlestrop*) but almost immediately turn right, off road to go through wooden kissing gate (sign - *Macmillan Way*). Almost immediately go through second wooden kissing gate and head across field, first following slightly sunken grassy track. Then aim just to right of cricket field fence, which soon becomes visible. Skirt left around cricket field fence and aim for large wooden gate. Go through wooden kissing gate to right of large gate and bear right to go up sloping, wooded path with wooden fences on both sides. Through wooden kissing gate to right of large metal gate to continue up pathway, now with walls on both sides. Pass old rectory on left and church up to right as we enter **Adlestrop**. Bear right on to public road and

The Fox Inn, Oddington

follow this as it bends to left (*leaving the course of the Macmillan Way*). Turn right at T-junction by useful wooden seat, with small shop along to left (*turn left here if you wish to look at the old Adlestrop Station sign with the well-known verse by Edward Thomas displayed above it, in a small bus shelter*). Turn left to follow road by Manor Farm House on right.

(C) At end of village, turn right at T-junction on to slightly busier road. Go along right-hand side of road and well before top of slope, turn right, off road to go over stile into belt of woodland (sign - *Public Footpath*). Turn left and soon bear right to follow path along belt of woodland, going parallel with road that we have just left. Soon ignore gate to right and follow path as it gently bears to right near top of slope. Ignore path going off at right-angles to left and keep parallel with road (not too easy to spot). At end of wood go through small wooden gate beside large wooden gate and turn left **with care** to go beside the ever-busy A436. Almost immediately cross the A436 **with very great care** and

Adlestrop Church

20

continue along its right-hand side.

(D) Where minor road comes in from left pass entrance gates on right and after 30 paces turn right to go through small wooden gate beside large one and keep on path through woodland. Soon, on meeting cross-fence at end of wood, turn right to go along path to right of this fence. Bear left to go along well-surfaced drive leading to **Daylesford** estate. Interesting large sculpture in field down to right and almost

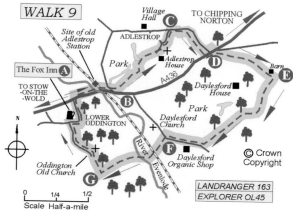

opposite this, bear left, off drive, onto wide farm road between wooden fences. At end of fenced road bear right to go over stone bridge and follow track through attractive woodland area. Over crossing of estate roads and follow better-surfaced road into impressive estate yard.

(E) At end of large barn on left, turn right to go down surfaced estate road (sign - *Gardens*). Pass Estate Office on right and keep straight down road. Pass layby on left. Pass house with extensive walled garden to right and follow this wall on our right as it bends to right. Pass wood on right. At end of estate road turn right **with great care** onto busy minor public road. Walk along this road with care facing oncoming traffic. **Daylesford** Organic Shop (with restaurant), with extensive car park, on left. Very slight glimpse of the Daylesford mansion through farm gateway on right.

Old station sign, Adlestrop

(F) At entrance to minute **Daylesford** village turn left, off road, to go through kissing gate and down right-hand edge of field with hedge to right. At end of field go through small wooden gate and turn right onto surfaced farm road. Over bridge crossing railway line and follow farm road as it bends to right and then to left. Over second bridge, this one crossing the infant River Evenlode. Where farm road bends to left go through small wooden gate on right and immediately turn left, to go up left-hand edge of field, parallel with farm road, now beyond hedge over to left. Turn left in corner of field to go through large metal gate and immediately turn right on to farm road. But after 10 paces turn right to go through small metal gate. Now keep along bottom, right-hand edge of field and turn left in corner to go up right-hand edge of field. Ignore first large metal gate on right and keep up field with fenced wood soon on right. At top of field go through small wooden gate into narrow belt of woodland.

(G) Soon turn right onto track with woodland belt on right. Pass **Oddington** old church on right - well worth visiting. Track now becomes surfaced public road. Enter **Oddington** village and turn right at T-junction. Arrive at the Fox Inn, on left, thus completing Walk 9 **(A)**.

WALK 10

LITTLE COMPTON - CHASTLETON - LITTLE COMPTON

Due to the muddy condition of part of our route between Points D and E, it is suggested that this walk is more suitable in the summer months.

Start from - The Red Lion Inn
Little Compton
GL56 0RT
Tel 01608 674 397
Length of walk: 6 miles
Approximate time: 3 hours

(A) Start from the Red Lion Inn, **Little Compton**, by turning left out of its car park, immediately ignoring cul-de-sac road to left and keeping along footpath on left-hand side of road soon passing converted chapel on left. Go straight, not right at road junction near phone box on left. Pass entrance gate to lovely old manor house on left and almost immediately go straight, not left at road junction (but walk to left if you wish to visit church). Pass entrance to Rivington Glebe on left. Ignore Drivers Lane on left and keep straight on up road. Where road bends sharply to left turn right to go up grassy track with hedge to left and wire fence to right following bridleway waymark. Where bridleway soon veers to left, bear right through large metal gate following footpath waymark's direction to go across top corner of field. Soon meet hedgeline and then bear right to go along top of field with hedge now on immediate left. Go through wide gap in cross-hedge and keep along left-hand edge of field with hedge to immediate left.

(B) At end of field go over stile and turn left to **walk with care** beside the busy A44 road. Initially keep to left-hand side of road but watch carefully for stile in hedge over to right just before house on right. Cross road **with very great care** and go over stile. Go down narrow path passing wooden shed on left before going over second stile. Go quietly along right-hand edge of garden and small orchard beyond. Through gap or over stile to its right and keep in same direction across small field. Over yet another stile and veer slightly left to go diagonally up across large sloping field. Fine views opening up behind us. Look for stile in wire fence, go over this and veer well to the right to follow waymark direction across next field and locate bridge in hollow, crossing very small stream. Over this bridge and follow

Dovecote at Chastleton

waymark's direction up across narrow sloping field and then go across a second bridge to immediate right of large metal gate. Go up field initially aiming just to right of Hill Farm's farmhouse. Turn left through metal gate and go quietly up farmyard with low barn to left and farmhouse now over to right. Keep up left-hand side of roadway between wall and wooden fence. Go through small wooden gate onto surfaced farm drive.

(C) At top of farm drive turn right with care onto partly unfenced public road. (*You have briefly joined the route of the* **Macmillan Way**.) Fine views ahead right. Pass entrance drive to Chastleton Hill, an attractive farmhouse down to right. Through large wooden gate beside cattle-grid and bear right onto slightly busier road. Pass entrance to National Trust's car park for Chastleton House. (*If you are visiting the house you can turn left here and walk along fields to the left of our road.*) Keep along road - good view of attractive dovecote over to left. Pass Chastleton Church on right and Chastleton House just beyond - don't miss a visit here. Follow road as it bends round to right (*now leaving* *the course of the* **Macmillan Way** *which goes to left up an avenue of fine trees on its way to distant Dorset).* Keep down road passing side of Chastelton House, up to right.

(D) Beyond post box on left turn left following *Restricted Byway* sign. Follow byway as it bends to left and then to right in yard. Soon ignore footpath sign to left and keep straight

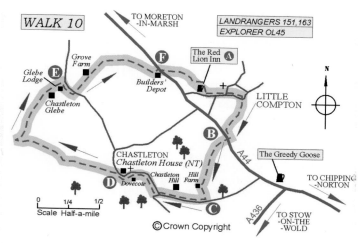

down byway. Pass modern barns on left and surface soon starts to deteriorate. Keep on track as it bends slightly near small electricity warning sign on right. At crossing of tracks, turn right onto narrower track (still classified as a Restricted Byway). Now very muddy and much used by horse-riders. Bear right and immediately bear left crossing small stream. Leave wooded area and emerge into field. Keep following track along right-hand edge of field. At end of field go through large metal gate onto more pronounced track and pass wood on right and hedge on left. At end of wood veer slightly right to join surfaced drive with entrance to Chastelton Glebe back to right.

(E) Just beyond Glebe Lodge on right, turn right **with care** onto public road. Soon, after passing houses on right, turn left down driveway of Grove Farm (sign - *Footpath to Little Compton 1½ miles*). Pass Little Grove (house) on right and veer right to go to right of low stone building. Go over stile just beyond and straight across small paddock and through large metal gate. Go along right-hand edge of next field and over stile below large tree. Go down right-hand edge of next field and through wooden kissing gate. Cross horse gallop with care and over stile. Keep in same direction down next field with hedge to immediate right. Through large metal gate and veer well to right following waymark's direction to cross large field. Through large metal gate (*possibly off its hinges!*) in fence-line and keep in same direction across next large field, aiming for its far right-hand corner. Go through large metal gate and keep along left-hand edge of field with tree-sheltered stream close to left. Ignore large gateway on left leading across stream and keep straight on. Before reaching end of field turn left to go over wooden footbridge and follow narrow path skirting to left of builders' depot with containers much in evidence.

(F) Turn right **with great care** onto narrow pathway beside the busy A44. Go beside A44 with great care and soon start to look for possibly part-concealed stile in hedge on opposite side of road. Cross road with great care and go over stile. Now veer right to go across bottom corner of field. Through gap in cross-hedge and veer right following waymark direction. At far edge of field go over wooden bridge crossing small stream and turn left to follow path with ditch to left and wooden fence to right. Where there is a footbridge to left, turn right to go down grassy walk. Soon join surfaced roadway at entry to **Little Compton**. Turn right with care onto wider road and then turn right into the car park of the Red Lion Inn, thus completing Walk 10 **(A)**.

23

WALK 11

WHICHFORD - WHICHFORD WOOD -
MARGETT'S HILL - WHICHFORD

(A) Turn right, out of the car park of the Norman Knight Inn, **Whichford**, to go along path on right-hand side of road. Almost immediately bear left at road junction by War Memorial and bus shelter, both opposite, and use path on right-hand side of road. Pass elegant Whichford House on right and church just beyond, also on right. At end of road turn left into Roman Row.

Start from - The Norman Knight Inn,
Whichford,
CV36 4PE
Tel 01608 684 621
Length of walk: 5 miles
Approximate time: 2½ hours

At end of Roman Row go through kissing gate ahead and possibly over small stile just beyond. At far end of hedge on right, turn right and head up bank aiming for gate at edge of wood. Through this metal kissing gate, to right of wooden gate and follow path up steep bank in wood. At top of path emerge from wood and turn right to go along wood's outer edge. On meeting cross-hedge bear right, back into wood and bear left to join wide woodland path. Eventually veer slightly left to follow track which has just entered wood from our left. Initially follow track within the very edge of wood, but soon bear right to follow track as it gradually drops down into still-wooded valley. Just beyond bottom of valley, go straight, not left. (*This point stands at the junction of two long-distance paths, the Macmillan Way and Shakespeare's Way.*) Almost immediately bear left onto better-surfaced track and follow this as it climbs out of valley.

Outside the Norman Knight Inn, Whichford

(B) At top of track go through large metal gate and turn right **with great care** onto public road. Go along right-hand side of road and soon turn left to go along surfaced drive (sign - *Margett's Hill Barn*). Pass stone cottage on left and converted Barn on right. Keep down track with wall on left and fence on right. At end of low mound on right turn right and go along path with fence to immediate right. At end of fence turn left by trees on right to join track which soon bends to right. Keep along this track with hedge to immediate left. At large gap where three fields meet turn left to go down right-hand edge of field with hedge to immediate right. At next gap, where three fields also meet, turn right to go along right-hand edge of field with hedge to immediate right. Pass small plantation on right and keep to immediate left of its edge and hedge beyond. Keep to immediate left of house to go through small wooden gate and ---

(C) --- Turn right with care onto public road. After 30 paces turn left to go through large wooden gates. Now bear left to keep well clear of house up to the right, but then veer right to go through wooden kissing gate in garden boundary ahead. Immediately turn left and then bear right to go over new stile and go diagonally down across field aiming for waymark to the right of large oak tree. Over waymarked style below oak tree and cross field diagonally aiming for small metal gate in group of willow trees. At the bottom of field go to the right of enclosed wire meshed pen and over small wooden bridge and through kissing gate. Bear slightly left to go down left hand edge of field with hedge on immediate left. Go through kissing gate beneath oak tree and veer half right to go across corner of field aiming for a waymarked gap in hedge. (if in doubt follow hedge round outside of this small corner to waymark) .Go over small wooden bridge, through a small metal gate and turn left to follow hedge down to small derelict barn on right and go through Bristol Gate onto road (A Bristol gate is a large metal gate with a small pedestrian gate set in it - we shall encounter more of these) ---

(D) --- go across public road **with great care** and through large metal gate with cattle-grid - **take care!**. Keep along farm track with farm buildings of Lanes Farm initially up to right. Where track bends to right turn right to go through Bristol gate.

Go along right-hand edge of field with hedge to right. Through metal kissing gate at right-hand end of cross-hedge and go straight across field with hedge about 20 paces to right. Through Bristol gate and keep in same direction across field. Through Bristol gate and keep in same direction across next field. Through metal kissing gate just to left of a power-pole and keep in same direction across field.

(E) Through metal kissing gate, cross track just beyond and then go diagonally across field aiming well to left of solitary oak tree. Through metal kissing gate just to left of large gate. Keep in approximately the same direction to go down bank aiming just to left of solitary oak tree. At bottom of field go through small metal gate, over substantial footbridge crossing stream. Turn right to go along bottom of bank with trees to right. Through Bristol gate and follow waymark's direction to go along top of bank. Pass oak tree on right and soon bear right where hedge bends to left, to go down grassy track into valley bottom. Veer right in valley bottom to go over possibly muddy stone `bridge' over very small tributary stream and up steep bank just beyond. Just beyond top of bank, go through metal gate into wood. Now going parallel to main stream well below, with inner edge of wood to left. Through small metal gate and keep in same direction, immediately re-entering wood. Eventually drop down on woodland path and at bottom, veer left through gap to go into field. Go along valley field, veering left, above stream to avoid possibly boggy area. At end of valley field, with house ahead, turn right to go over concrete bridge and up slope.

(F) Through metal gate and wooden gate and turn left **with care** onto busy public road at entry to **Whichford**. Now go along road, going up bank and passing entrance to Whichford Pottery on left. Bear left by War Memorial and turn left into the Norman Knight Inn, thus completing Walk 11 **(A)**.

View from our path beyond Whichford

25

WALK 12

SIBFORD GOWER -EPWELL - SIBFORD GOWER

(A) Set out from the Wykham Arms, **Sibford Gower**, by turning right, out of its car park and going along right-hand side of public road, immediately passing plaque on left marking house once occupied by Frank Lascelles (1874 - 1934), the once well-known 'Pageant Master'. Over crossroads (follow sign - *Epwell*). Soon turn left up onto Backside Lane

> Start from - The Wykham Arms, Sibford Gower, OX15 5RX
> Tel 01295 788 808
> Length of walk: 5 miles
> Approximate time: 2½ hours

(also signed - *Bridleway*). Keep straight out of village on this lane eventually passing farm and farmhouse on left. Through two large metal gates and go down right-hand edge of field with hedge to immediate right. But well before end of field turn down right by single tree on right and go through large metal gate. Keep down left-hand edge of next field and at bottom of field go through large metal gate, over bridge crossing stream. Go steeply up track with trees on both sides.

(B) At end of track turn right onto an ancient green road known as **Ditchedge Lane**, which forms the boundary between Warwickshire (on our left) and Oxfordshire (on our right). (*Now on the course of the **Macmillan Way**.*) Keep on Ditchedge Lane ignoring bridleway to left. Through small wooden gate to left of large metal gate and keep in same direction going beside busy B4035 **with great care**. Where road bends to right, go straight ahead to rejoin green lane overhung with trees and now known as Beggars' Lane. Through small metal gate to left of large metal gate. Watch out carefully for partly-concealed base of radio mast in bushes to right and after 110 paces turn right to go over wooden stile leaving Beggars' Lane and the course of the **Macmillan Way**. Go across centre of field following waymark's direction.

Ditchedge Lane

(C) Through large metal gate and turn right with care onto busy minor road. After 60 paces turn left to go through large metal gate and go down left-hand edge of field with hedge on immediate left. Through large metal gate and keep along left-hand edge of field. At bottom corner of field turn right onto well-used path and after 30 paces turn left to go through tall wooden gate and go down left-hand edge of next field. Keep in same direction down narrow pathway with hedge to left and low garden fence to right. Through small metal gate and turn right on to public road at our entry to **Epwell**. Follow road as it bends to left and after 30 paces turn right to go up track with churchyard wall on left (sign - *Chandlers' Arms*). Pass gate to churchyard on left (*there are two useful benches in the churchyard*) and keep in same direction on to grassy pathway along left-hand edge of field with houses down to left. Follow path as it bends round to right and at its end turn left **with care** on to public road and pass the Chandlers' Arms (*Tel: 01295 780 747 - Post Code: OX15 6LH*) on left.

(D) Almost immediately fork right, off road and then turn right at x-rds of tracks to go through large wooden waymarked gate to immediate right of un-named house. Bear left immediately beyond gate and follow left-hand edge of field with garden fence initially to left. Soon go on grassy track with hedge on left and small plantation to right. Soon go through small metal gate and follow bridleway sign ahead and ignoring

Darcy Dalton Way waymark (signed to right). Keep along left-hand edge of field and at its far corner ignore bridleway waymarks and turn very sharp right to go up left-hand edge of field. After 40 paces turn left to go through metal gate and then left again to go down farm track. On approaching Chilaway Farmhouse and outbuildings (name not indicated) veer left and then right passing power-pole with transformer on immediate left. At end of farmyard go through large metal gate and keep along right-hand edge of field with hedge on immediate right. Pass large pond on left and start to climb gently. Through large metal gate and veer slightly right to follow waymark's direction across centre of very large field. On reaching brow aim just to right of farm buildings well ahead.

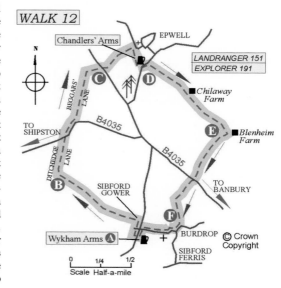

Well before end of field go to immediate right of narrow belt of woodland parallel with our route. Go along track, parallel with and to immediate right of this woodland.

(E) On reaching modest farmhouse on left (part of Blenheim Farm), turn right, off track and head across large field, aiming just to right of converted barns well ahead. Cross surfaced drive keeping well to right of converted barns and go steeply up right-hand edge of field with hedge and trees to immediate right. Before reaching top, stop to look back at fine views over open country beyond Blenheim Farm. At top of hill go through gateway and cross busy B4035 **with great care**. Over stile beside metal gate (sign - *Burdrop*) and go straight across field following waymark direction. Over stile and go to left to keep along left-hand edge of field with fence to immediate left. Follow this edge, going down into valley with hedge and trees to left. Over stile beside metal gate and go along right-hand edge of next field with hedge to immediate right.

(F) Just before meeting house ahead, go over wooden stile and then bear right onto public road at entry to Burdrop. Turn right at road junction (sign - *Sibford Gower*). Now entering **Sibford Gower** and pass church and then school, both on left. Turn left at x-rds (sign - *Temple Mill*) and soon arrive at the Wykham Arms, on left, thus completing Walk 12 **(A)**.

Open Country beyond Blenheim Farm

27

WALK 13

SHENINGTON - EPWELL - SHENINGTON

Start from - The Bell Inn,
Shenington,
OX15 6NQ
Tel 01295 670 274
Length of walk: 5 miles
Approximate time: 2½ hours

(A) Set out from the Bell Inn, **Shenington**, by turning right, out of its front door. Cross public road **with care**, to right of bus shelter and go along minor road across middle of wide village green. At end of green continue along road passing Mulberry Cottage, Green End Cottage and Mizpah Cottage, all on right. At end of road, immediately beyond Honeysuckle Cottage, on left, go down grassy path to go through two large metal gates (sign - *Footpath*). After ten paces turn left to go over stone stile and wooden stile (sign - *Historic Village Trail* - henceforth referred to here as *HVT*). Go diagonally right, down across field and in bottom right-hand corner go through large metal gate (sign - *HVT*) and immediately turn left to go down left-hand edge of field. After 50 paces bear right (sign - *HVT*) and go diagonally across field. Over stile and stone footbridge, crossing the infant Sor Brook, a small tributary of the Cherwell, which itself flows into the Thames at Oxford.

(B) Immediately go through small metal gate and veer right to go up bank, ignoring *HVT* sign to left (*But turn left if you wish to visit Brook Cottage Garden - see* **Alkerton**). Turn right at top of bank, keeping parallel with brook, well below. Go through small, dilapidated wooden gate (might have been replaced!). Now go along field following contour with brook well down to right, soon going below low-voltage power-line on a more defined track. Where track starts to bend round to left, turn right to go down slope to left of bushy area. Go along wooden walkway and bridge in valley, and through small metal gate. Keep straight across slope of next field with brook still down to right, soon coming closer to bushy area on right. Go over stile in cross-fence and keep in same direction across next sloping field. Go over another stile in next cross-fence and still keep close to right-hand edge of field. In right-hand corner of field go over stile in bushy area with stream down to right and keep along right-hand edge of next field with brook now closely down to right.

(C) Soon turn right to cross brook and go through small wooden gate, joining a bridleway. Head across field following waymark's direction and at end of field go over substantial wooden bridge crossing the Sor Brook. Beyond bridge, go though small

On the Green at Shenington

metal gate and head up field, soon crossing horse-gallop and keep on up well-worn bridleway path. Go beneath high-voltage power-line as path becomes steeper. Near top go over horse-gallop and through small metal gate just beyond. Keep straight across field heading to the immediate left of barns (shown on map as Field Barn). Keep to immediate left of barns and veer left to join track along right-hand edge of field with

28

hedge to immediate right. At end of field veer right to follow track through gap in hedge. Now keep on track on left-hand side of next field, but where track turns left, go straight ahead across field aiming just to right of twin low-voltage power-poles. Small bumpy hills ahead - Yarn Hill to left and Epwell Hill to right. Through large metal gate in cross-hedge and keep in same direction across next field aiming for wide gap in cross-hedge. Through this wide gap and keep in same direction across next field.

(D) Through large metal gate and, at inverted T-junction of public roads beyond, keep in same direction to go along right-hand side of public road **with great care** (sign - *Epwell*). (But turn right to go along public road for about

half-a-mile, if you wish to link on to Point **(F)** to make a short-cut return to Shenington.) On Main Route keep along road signed to Epwell until reaching barns on left. Now turn right, off road just before barns on left (sign - *Footpath - Epwell*) - to go through wide gap in hedge. Go diagonally across large field aiming for far left-hand corner. Over small wooden bridge in corner of field and bear right to go along right-hand edge of field with hedge to immediate right. Go below low-voltage power-line and almost immediately veer left to keep down right-hand edge of field ignoring small metal gate to right. Through gap in cross-hedge and keep down next field with hedge still to immediate right. Pass rough area with young trees on left before going

Epwell Church

over small bridge crossing stream and through metal kissing-gate. Bear right to keep along right-hand edge of field with fence to immediate right. Pass house on right at entry to Epwell and ---

(E) --- Through metal kissing gate and turn left to go along road into village. (*But turn right if you wish to miss out Epwell and refer to Point E1 below.*) Soon cross small bridge to left of ford and continue up road. Turn left at T-junction in centre of village (sign - *Banbury*) and go along road. Turn right at next T-junction (sign - *The Sibfords*). Keep up road passing attractive green on left and the Chandlers' Arms on right (*Tel: 01295 780 747 - Post Code: OX15 6LH*). After 40 paces beyond inn turn right, initially onto wide track and then through gap to left of inn's garden onto wide grass headland path along right-hand edge of field (sign - *To the Church*). Keep along right-hand edge of field with walls to immediate right soon bearing left and then onto path between hedge on left and fence on right. Soon turn right to go through metal gate into churchyard. Keep

Ford at Epwell

on path through churchyard with church down to left. Pass useful bench and then go through wooden gate and keep straight along road at T-junction which we passed after entering the village. Now retrace route to go down road to go beside ford and ---

(E1) --- and pass kissing gate on right, just beyond (*this is common with Point **E**, where we entered the village*). Fork right by small green on left, passing converted barn on right, pass sign *Birds Lane* on right and then go through large wooden gate (sign - *Footpath - Shenington*). Go quietly across mown area of garden keeping to its left-hand side. Veer left at end of garden and go over stile. Go up left-hand side of small field, through small metal gate and across next small field. Through another small metal gate and go across middle of field, going between Epwell Hill on left and Yarn Hill on right. On meeting hedge coming in from left, veer right to go to its immediate right. At far end of field go through large metal gate and keep down left-hand side of next field. Go under high-and low-voltage power-lines and keep in same direction down short track.

(F) Turn left **with care** onto public road (*we are joined here by the short-cut from Point **D**). After about 40 paces turn right to go over stile (sign - *Shenington*) and go diagonally across field aiming for low-voltage power-pole just to right of clump of trees beyond. Drop down into valley beyond power-pole and go over stile and footbridge crossing stream.

(G) At bottom right-hand corner of field go over stile and immediately turn right to soon go over another stile, to right-hand side of large metal gate. Go up sloping field well to right of possible fence aiming for stile which soon becomes visible in possibly temporary cross-fence. Follow grassy track as it bends round to left with fence above to left. Through large metal gate in valley bottom and go straight ahead to climb steep curving track. At top of bank go through large metal gate and keep on track along right-hand edge of field. At end of field go over stile to right of large metal gate and initially keep on track as it veers to left. But almost immediately veer right, off track and go down field into valley aiming just to left of line of willow trees. Go over small bridge and stile and go steeply up field with fence to immediate right. At top of bank go over stile and turn right **with care** onto public road at the entrance to **Shenington**. Keep along right-hand side of road and soon arrive at village green. Turn left onto minor road by bus shelter and arrive at the Bell Inn, on left, thus completing Walk 13 **(A)**.

Cottages at Epwell

WALK 14

OXHILL - PILLERTON PRIORS - PILLERTON HERSEY - OXHILL

(A) Set out from the Peacock Inn, **Oxhill**, turning left out of its yard or front door and going along village street, keeping on left-hand path beside road. Pass Village Hall on left, then bear right at T-junction and almost immediately turn left onto farm track.(*We shall keep on this track for about half-a-mile.*) Ignore kissing gate on right (we shall come out of here on our return journey to Oxhill). Pass farm on left. Pass second group of farm buildings on left and go through large metal gate. After gate the track becomes less definite and more grassy and we keep in same direction along right-hand edge of open field. Through large metal gate and keep in same direction along right-hand edge of smaller field.

(B) Through large wooden gate and after 15 paces turn left to go up grassy track - initially plantation on right and bushes on left. Through wooden gates and keep up hill with young woodland to right and mature trees to left. Pass large pond down to right and through large, obliquely-placed wooden gate. Keep up slope in same direction to go through second large wooden gate. Keep in same direction, with enlarged Oxhill Hill House soon visible down to right. Now head for left-hand end of wooden fencing and go over small stile to left of fenced enclosure. Now turn right to go along surfaced drive and over cross-roads of drives onto less well-surfaced farm road. Now follow down this farm road as it bends to left.

(C) Well beyond this bend turn right through large metal gate and go straight down track passing two metal containers on right. These are used as shelters for horses. This track is deeply rutted and can be difficult to walk along in winter. Where track veers to left, go straight ahead through small wooden gate on right and keep in same direction across large field first aiming for wide gap in hedge far ahead. Soon head just to right of another container and go through small metal gate just to its right. Now veer slightly right across narrow field to head for wooden footbridge. Go over this bridge, crossing the Wagtail Brook. Now go across next field aiming for metal gate in wide hedge gap. Through this "Bristol gate" (*a Bristol gate is large metal gate with a small one within it and is for the express use of walkers*) and veer right to go up across large field aiming for large gap in sporadic hedgeline probably with a small tree in the middle of it. At top of field go through another Bristol gate and keep in same direction along left-hand edge of field with fence to immediate left. Now go over stile into small spinney at the effective entry

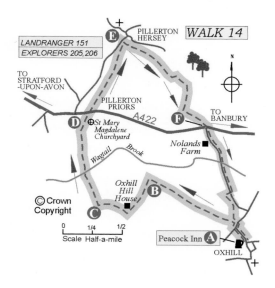

LANDRANGER 151
EXPLORERS 205,206

TO STRATFORD-UPON-AVON

PILLERTON HERSEY

WALK 14

PILLERTON PRIORS

St Mary Magdalene Churchyard

A422

TO BANBURY

Nolands Farm

Wagtail Brook

Oxhill Hill House

© Crown Copyright

Peacock Inn

OXHILL

0 1/4 1/2
Scale Half-a-mile

31

to **Pillerton Priors**. Go through spinney, over second stile and keep to right-hand edge of farmyard. Now keep in same direction to go down surfaced road. Pass entrance gate to **Pillerton Priors** churchyard on right - church destroyed by fire in 1666 and not replaced.

(D) On reaching small triangular green veer right and **cross busy A422 with very great care** and go over stile on far side of road. Go along left-hand edge of field passing house and barns beyond on left. Through small wooden gate, pass houses on left and through metal kissing gate. Now keep down right-hand edge of field and eventually go through metal kissing gate. Keep to right-hand edge of field going between hedge on right and wooden fence on left. Through metal kissing gate and again keep along right-hand edge of field. Through small wooden gate and keep along right-hand edge of field. Through small wooden gate into minute spinney and immediately through metal gate into large sloping field. Good view ahead, which, in winter, includes Pillerton Hersey's church tower. Go down middle of field aiming for small gate in cross-fence with new hedge. Through this small metal gate and keep in same direction across next, smaller, field. Through metal kissing gate in cross-hedge and turn left to go around left-hand edge of field. Pass old metal fuel tank on left and now, on the edge of **Pillerton Hersey**, ---

(E) --- Veer right to join track along lower, left-hand edge of field. *(But turn left to cross busy minor road with care and go on to grassy path opposite if you wish to visit **Pillerton Hersey** church.)* Keep on track as it first bends to right and then to left, ignoring two stiles on left. Now on long track with hedge to left. Eventually keep on track as it turns to left and go through gap in hedge before turning right onto roughly-surfaced farm drive. Pass tree-shaded pond on left. Pleasant open view of wood up to left. Where drive bends slightly to left, turn right onto farm track going through large metal gate following blue bridleway waymark. Keep straight up track passing cart shed on right and through small wooden gate. At top of track turn left to go through small wooden gate and go along left-hand edge of field with hedge on immediate left. Woodland visible ahead. Follow field edge as it veers round to right, with trees now to left.

(F) At end of field go through small wooden gate, **cross the busy A422 with great care** and go onto minor public road opposite (*Sign - Nolands Farm*). Through wooden gate to right of cattle-grid. Good views ahead, including **Brailes Hill** with its clump of trees, when road starts to descend. Entry to Newborough Farm on left. Avenue of trees leading to Nolands Farm on right. Go carefully to left of cattle grid. Now heading across open country on minor road. View of Edge Hill opening up to left. *Just before trees on left pass the site of a Roman villa on right - nothing visible, but a mosaic floor was excavated here and then re-covered some years ago.* Pass sewage works on left. Turn right, off road, just before reaching cattle-grid and go along left-hand edge of field before turning left to cross small wooden bridge over stream. Now veer left across field following waymark's direction, which is just to the right of the tallest tree ahead. Over wooden bridge re-crossing the Wagtail Brook and keep in same direction, close to the left-hand edge of field, passing garden and large barn. Ignore gates to left and keep in same direction. At end of field, through wooden kissing gate and turn left onto farm track to enter outskirts of **Oxhill**, re-joining our early route out of the village. At end of track veer right to go straight across public road junction (*Sign - Village Centre*) and go into village, keeping on path on right of road. Pass Village Hall on right and soon arrive back at the Peacock Inn, thus completing Walk 14 **(A)**.

Near Pillerton Priors

WALK 15

SHENINGTON - TYSOE - SHENINGTON

(A) Start from the Bell Inn, **Shenington**, turning left with your back to its front door, and going approximately north-west and forking right just beyond it to go along Kenhill Road, passing several attractive stone cottages, some thatched. At end of village keep straight up gravel roadway, go through large wooden gate and keep up rougher track in same direction. Over stile beside metal

Start from - The Bell Inn,
Shenington,
OX15 6NQ
Tel 01295 670 274
Length of walk: 5¾ miles
Approximate time: 3 hours

gate and keep straight ahead on track. Now in the Shenington Airfield area, crossing old aircraft runway. Keep along track with fence to left and possible gliders in field beyond it. Through metal gate and cross another runway to go on to track with fence to immediate left. Through gateway and keep on track with fence now on both sides. Through metal gate and veer slightly left to go across field. Through wide gap at end of field and go along left-hand edge of next field with hedge to immediate left. At end of field go through gap and almost immediately go through metal gate into Sugarswell Farm area, bearing left onto surfaced road with barns to right. Keep along attractive tree-lined farm drive.

(B) At end of Sugarswell Farm's drive go straight across busy minor road with great care and through small metal gate beside large metal gate. (*But if you wish to do the shorter Shenington Circuit, turn right here to walk with care along road for just under a quarter-of-a-mile, as far as Point (E) to join path leading back to Shenington.*) Now go along green lane with hedges on both sides - once used as part of Shenington Airfield. At end of green lane veer slightly left to go onto path into open woodland, crossing remains of old aircraft dispersal point - hence the apparent green lane. Keep to left-hand of paths to enter wood and keep into wood along its inside left-hand edge. Path now level for some distance but then drops steeply down. **Take great care on this steep descent, especially after rain**. At bottom of wood go over stile and go straight down across field aiming for gap in cross-hedge. Over stile in gap with horse-trough to left. Keep down field with left-hand hedge about 20 paces to left. Aim well to left

of Tysoe church tower, visible ahead. Over stile in cross-hedge and keep down field with left-hand hedge and stream about 20 paces to left. Pass house over to left beyond stream. In far left-hand corner of field drop steeply down to cross stile and small bridge. Go up short pathway

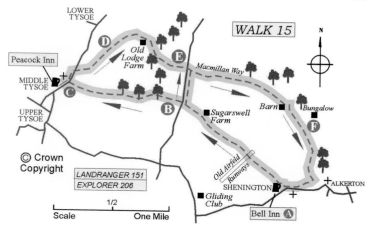

33

and bear right on to minor road at entry to **Tysoe.**

(C) Turn tight **with care,** out of Peacock Lane, onto busier road and cross to footpath on far side. (*But turn left if you wish to visit the Peacock Inn in the centre of village - Tel: 01295 680 338 - Post Code CV35 0SE.*) Pass church on left, Church Farm on right and Church Farm Court cul-de-sac on left. Immediately beyond, turn right, to go across road and through kissing gate to left of second large metal gate and

Cottages near the Bell Inn, Shenington

immediately beyond 30 mph de-restriction sign. Go diagonally left across field following Centenary Way waymark. (*We shall now follow the* **Centenary Way** *across several fields.*) On meeting hedge protruding from left, veer slightly left to go along left-hand edge of field with hedge now on immediate left. At waymark post follow waymark direction and veer right, across field, aiming for gap in cross-hedge. Through this wide gap and go along left-hand edge of next field.

(D) In left-hand corner of field, go through metal kissing gate and initially keep on left-hand edge of field. But soon veer right to aim for gateway in top, left-hand corner of field. In this corner, go through metal kissing gate in hedge to left of gateway. Follow up right-hand edge of field and go through unusual metal gate. Go straight ahead on signed footpath (yellow arrow) ignoring Centenary Way waymark aiming to left (*thus leaving the Centenary Way*). Now aim just to left of Old Lodge Farm's garden fence. Turn right by small green shed on right and go through large metal gate. Go to immediate left of farmhouse and follow up surfaced drive as it curves to left and enters woodland. Near top of hill, pass footpaths to right and left, that from the left being used by the **Macmillan Way,** which joins us. (*We shall now follow the* **Macmillan Way** *for the rest of our route.*) Keep on surfaced road as it levels out.

Shenington Church

(E) Cross busy minor road **with great care** and go straight along grassy track directly opposite, with some

34

trees to its left. Good southward views opening up ahead. We have now crossed the Severn-Thames watershed and all streams beyond this point will be feeding into tributaries of the Thames. Through large metal gate and veer slightly left, keeping about 20 paces away from right-hand edge of field. Soon start to drop down towards valley and pass sporadic line of trees extending to our left. Through small wooden gate in cross-hedge and keep down next field still keeping about 20 paces away from hedge to right, but then veer left in valley to go over concrete `bridge'. Bear right beyond bridge to aim for wide gap in tall hedge ahead. Through large metal gate in gap and veer right following **Macmillan Way** waymark to go along right-hand edge of very large field with willow trees to right. At end of field go through gap in cross-hedge with oak tree to immediate left and then veer left to pass well to the left of low, stone barn.

(F) Soon bear right to join track with wood to immediate left. At end of wood go through large metal gate and go across field on grassy track. At end of field go through gateway in wide gap with hunting rail to right. Keep in same direction aiming to left of two groups of bushes ahead, and following grassy track. Bungalow soon visible back left. Keep on grassy track beyond bushes aiming for gateway in cross-hedge. Through gateway and keep on grassy track with long wood now up to left. Shenington's church tower now visible across valley ahead right. At end of field go through large metal gate in cross-fence and keep straight ahead for about 50 paces and then turn right to go down rough field and through gap in post and rail fence, veering left beyond it. Go through metal gate into possibly overgrown area and over small wooden bridge with small stile at its far end, crossing the Sor Brook. Now head up field to immediate left of group of poplar trees. Beyond poplars aim for top, right-hand corner of field and beyond it, go up narrow path between bushes to go through metal kissing gate. Turn right **with great care** to go up beside public road into village of **Shenington**. Pass church, up to left, and old school just beyond. Then bear right onto small road at entrance to large village green and pass bus shelter beneath trees, to arrive at the Bell Inn, thus completing Walk 15 **(A)**.

Our route beyond Point E

WALK 16

LOWER BRAILES - SUTTON-UNDER-BRAILES - STOURTON - CHERINGTON - LOWER BRAILES

(A) With your back to its front door, turn right from The George, **Lower Brailes**. Walk a few paces to the stone barn at the eastern end of the George and turn right onto footpath (sign - *Sutton-under-Brailes*). Go down path with high wall on right and iron fence to left. Over low stone stile. Go straight over x-rds of paths (sign - *Plough Lane*). Through small wooden gate, cross track and over

small stile. Go straight across field keeping just to left of single tree with waymark post just to its left. Pass drinking trough by hedge on left and after 25 paces turn left to go over stile in hedge. Now veer sharply right and head for stile in cross-fence over to right. Go over stile and keep in same direction across next field. Go over stile and small bridge in cross-hedge and keep in same direction aiming for left-hand end of projecting hedge. Through Bristol gate just beyond low-voltage power-pole and veer left to go up along left-hand edge of field. Buildings back, over to right are part of New Barn Farm.

(B) Go through another Bristol gate at far end of field and keep in same direction up across next field following waymark direction, almost immediately going to left of single ash tree. Go over stile and wooden bridge and veer left across corner of next field following waymark direction. Soon reach top edge of field and look carefully for un-waymarked gap on left. Go through this gap and turn right to go along right-hand edge of large field with tall, bushy hedge to immediate right. Keep along this field until reaching wide gap on right with track on right.

Brailes Church

(C) Bear right to go on track down side of hill slope, following well-concealed waymark on post to right. Very little sign of Rectory Farm which lies behind us, below path which we have been on. *We shall keep on this track until joining a road into Sutton-under-Brailes.* Keep steeply down on track, eventually passing restored building over to left, named on OS map as Oathill Hovel. Over stile beside large metal gate - hedges now on both sides of track. Pass small building beyond hedge on right. Ignore stile on right giving access to footpath across golf course, which is soon visible over to right. Track now goes gently upwards.

(D) Turn left **with care** on to public road at the entry to **Sutton-under-Brailes**. Go straight, not left, at road junction at entry to large village green (sign - *Burmington*). Now use path on right-hand edge of wide grass verge. Pass phone box on left and War Memorial over to left. Where road bends to right bear left across it and go down minor roadway across green following waymark direction. (*But go straight ahead beside road if you wish to visit the church.*) Well beyond green bear left immediately beyond dutch barn and go between it and large barns, now to right. Then turn right to go alongside back of large barns. At end of barns veer left to go through small metal gate into young woodland. At end of woodland go through another small metal gate and emerge into field. Keep in same direction, initially following line of power-poles but on meeting hedge coming in from left, turn

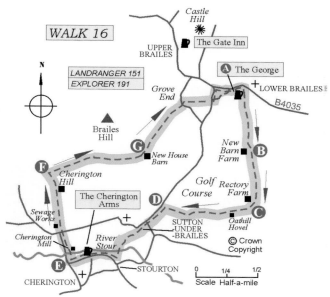

WALK 16

LANDRANGER 151
EXPLORER 191

left to go through metal kissing gate and bridge crossing stream. Veer right across field aiming well to right of low-voltage power-pole to go through kissing gate in cross-fence. Keep in same direction across next small field veering left beyond tennis court and wooden fence on left. Turn left to go through wooden kissing gate and go up across wide mown grassy area with houses to left. Turn right on to public road **with care** in **Stourton** . Initially use path on right-hand side of road but soon cross to left-hand side. Go straight, not left at road junction by small green at entry to **Cherington**. Pass Cherington Arms on right (*Tel: 01608 686 233 - Post Code CV36 5HS*). (*But turn left at far end of its car park opposite and go up path in far left-hand corner if you wish to walk across meadow to visit Cherington Church.*) Keep on beside road beyond Cherington Arms. Pass converted Cherington Mill on right and ---

Sutton-under-Brailes Church

(E) --- turn right at road T-junction (sign - *Burmington*) and go up road, soon crossing bridge over the infant River Stour. Pass entry to sewage works on left just beyond and start to climb steadily. At T-junction go straight ahead, leaving public road and go through wooden kissing gate to left of cattle-grid, on to private drive (house sign - *Cherington Hill*.) Go up surfaced drive, through wooden kissing gate to left of cattle-grid and pass converted buildings on right. Through third kissing gate beyond which drive starts to go up more steeply. Pass small pond on left and through yet another kissing gate to left of cattle-grid and now go straight up across very steep park-like field, leaving drive to wind up less steeply over to right. Through small gate and keep in same direction across field keeping just to right of fenced young plantation. A fine stone house over to right - this is Cherington Hill. Now at the very top of our climb up this shoulder of Brailes Hill from which there are outstanding views in many directions, especially southwards. Through wooden kissing gate and keep in same direction going along right-hand side of field with hedge to immediate right. There are now very fine open views over to the north and west.

(F) Well before reaching corner turn right to go through large metal gate and go straight along field with wooden fence to immediate right. Go through large metal gate and keep in same direction along narrow field with fences on both sides. Clump of trees on top of **Brailes Hill** ahead left. Splendid walking in this high country. Through small metal gate and go along field with hedge on immediate left. Through large metal

Cottage at Cherington

gate and go along left-hand edge of narrow field. Through small metal gate and, ignoring footpath signed to left and right, go straight ahead around right-hand edge of very large field following bridleway waymark, with hedge and trees to immediate right. This large open field stretches up towards the clump of trees near the summit of **Brailes Hill,** Shipston Country's favourite landmark. However it is not always visible from our path. Go through wide gap into next field and immediately go below ash tree. Previous headland has now become good grassy track, which is soon joined by better surfaced track coming in from the right. Follow track as it veers to left passing farm house and buildings down to right - shown as New House Barn on OS map.

(G) Where track turns down to right beyond farm buildings, go straight ahead through large metal gate (footpath waymarked - 61) and go along track with fence and hedge to immediate right. Brailes church tower now visible in valley, ahead right. Through large metal gate and go along left-hand edge of field with hedge to immediate left. At end of field go through small wooden gate into narrow bushy area overhung by trees. Eventually start to drop downwards. Ignore stile giving access to footpath on left and keep down path in bushy area. **Descend with great care** as this path is very uneven in places, slippery in wet conditions and may have one or two badger holes. Emerge onto grassy area with house on left, this being Grove End, the southern extremity of Upper Brailes. Turn left **with care** onto public road and immediately beyond house on right go over stile beside wooden gate. Go down short grassy path with fence to right and hedge to left. Over stile and veer slightly left to go down small field with young trees to left. Through small metal gate and keep in same direction across next field. Through small metal gate and down grassy path with hedges on both sides. Through small metal kissing gate and turn left **with care** onto public road at entry to **Lower Brailes**. Cross road to go along right-hand footpath beside it. Turn right at T-junction on to busy B4035 (sign - *Banbury*). Keep along right-hand footpath, but cross to left-hand side in dip to use left-hand footpath. At top of rise re-cross road to right-hand side and almost immediately arrive back at The George, thus completing Walk 16 (A).

WALK 17

THE GREEDY GOOSE - LITTLE ROLLRIGHT -

SALFORD - CORNWELL - THE GREEDY GOOSE

(A) Set out from the Greedy Goose, an inn once known as the Cross Hands, situated on the A44 between **Moreton-in-Marsh** and **Chipping Norton**, at its junction with the A436 from Stow-on-the-Wold. Turn right, out of the inn's car park **with very great care**, to walk along the right-hand verge of the very busy A44 (sign - *Evesham*). For safety's sake soon cross A44 to its left-hand side.

> Start from - The Greedy Goose,
> On A44 twixt Moreton-in-Marsh
> and Chipping Norton,
> GL56 0SP
> Tel 01608 646 551
> Length of walk: 7 miles
> Approximate time: 3½ hours

Where A44 starts to gently drop downwards, turn right, opposite minor road coming in from left, onto surfaced track (sign - *Macmillan Way*). Now on the course of the **Macmillan Way**. Keep on track passing farm buildings over to right. Beyond large hoppers on right go along left-hand edge of field with low wall to left. Through gap in corner of field below transformer on power-pole and along grassy track on right-hand edge of next field. At end of field go slightly left but keep along track along right-hand edge of next field with tall, bushy hedge to right.   Track starts to climb very gently and goes through gap into next field. At end of field watch carefully for path to go up through bushes to right before turning left to go along left-hand edge of field.

(B) At end of field bear slightly left to go through gap to left of large metal gate and turn right with care onto minor public road. Walk beside road with care almost immediately bearing left at bend.   Bear right following road at next bend, leaving the course of the **Macmillan Way** which goes straight ahead over small stone stile. Also **Shakespeare's Way** comes in over this same stone stile and we shall now follow its course as far as Salford.   Immediately beyond bend pass radio mast beyond bushes to right.   Pass quarry entrance on right. Go straight, not left at road junction (sign - *Rollright Stones*).

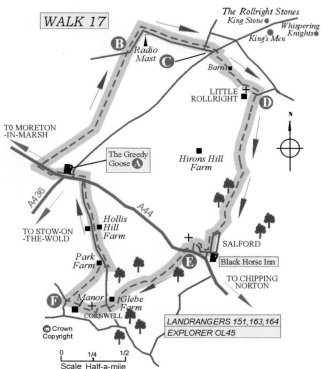

39

(C) Soon, go straight over road at T-junction ahead (**with great care**) and go over stile to left of gate (sign - *Footpath*). Go down track with hedge to left and fence to right. Fine views ahead. By farm buildings to left, keep on track as it bends to right and almost immediately bear left to go down track with trees on both sides. **Little Rollright** Church soon in view ahead. Turn left at T-junction of tracks in front of Little Rollright Church (*but go straight ahead and then left if you wish to visit this most attractive church*). Now follow surfaced drive around the edge of **Little Rollright** hamlet. Pass gateway to right and immediately beyond it bear right keeping on drive.

(D) Go through small metal gate beside large one with cattle-grid and turn right to go down driveway. After forty paces turn left to go down pathway with fences on both sides (signs - *Darcy Dalton Way* and *Shakespeare's Way*). Pass large farm building on left and veer slightly

Little Rollright Church

left to go up sunken pathway, soon crossing track and going uphill on path with hedge on left and fence on right and then bushes beyond. At top of hill go through two metal kissing gates and keep along right-hand edge of large field with hedge on immediate right. At end of field go through small wooden gate into wood. Follow defined path through wood and at its end, go over stile and through very small stream. Go along right-hand edge of field but well before reaching wood on right, turn right through large metal gate and immediately turn left to go along left-hand edge of field, thus keeping in same direction. Soon go through metal gate to enter wood and follow defined path through it. At end of wood go over stile and keep along left-hand edge of field to pass barns over to left. At end of field go over stile into edge of woodland and almost immediately over second stile into field. Go straight across field following waymark's direction and go over stile into very narrow belt of woodland. Soon turn left onto track and almost immediately turn right onto wider roadway to enter outskirts of **Salford** village. Fork right at x-rds by village green passing play area and picnic table on left. Immediately turn right by Chase Cottage up smaller road following waymark. (*But keep straight ahead if you wish to visit the Black Horse Inn - Tel: 01608 642 824 - Post Code: OX7 5YW.*) Over stile at end of road and after 30 paces turn left to go through wide gap. Go diagonally right, across field and go through metal kissing gate in far right hand corner. Go into churchyard and skirt around left-hand end of church to go through gate onto roadway (*those who have visited the Black Horse should re-join the route at this point*). Keep in same direction to go along path with fence to right and hedge to left.

((E) At end of path turn right **with great care** to go along right-hand verge of the very busy A44 road. Just beyond 50 mph sign cross road **with very great care** and go through gap in hedgeline (sign - *Cornwell*). Turn right on to grassy track to go parallel with road but well below it. Soon turn left keeping on grassy track with hedge on left and trees to right. (We shall follow this attractive green lane almost as far as Cornwell.) Pass wood on left, grassy track soon has hedges on both sides and grass is eventually replaced by a more solid surface. Large pond probably visible over to left. Bear left at junction of tracks following bridleway waymark. On meeting farm buildings bear left, then right, to go between them. At end of buildings aim slightly left to go onto surfaced track with house to its right. At T-junction of roadways turn right and after 40 paces turn left to go through small wooden gate (sign - *Footpath*). Go straight down left-hand edge of field to cross "bridge" over small stream (possibly dry in high summer). Up bank beyond and at its top go through gap on to grassy track with woodland on either side. Through metal kissing gate into **Cornwell's** churchyard and follow path around left-hand side of church. Pass church porch and leave churchyard through kissing gate. Go along pathway overhung by trees. At end of trees turn right through metal kissing gate and ignoring stile to right, look carefully for metal kissing gate ahead left, beyond short run of wooden fence. Through this kissing gate and turn right to go up narrow pathway to immediate left of hedge, with orchard to left.

(F) Through gap in hedge at end of orchard and turn right on to track with wood now to left and fence to right. (But turn left if you wish to explore **Cornwell** hamlet - much of it the creation of Clough Williams-Ellis.) Pass farm buildings on left and where track bends to left towards buildings, go straight ahead onto grassy track into wooded area. Over stile well to the right of large wooden gate. Keep in same direction down across large park-like field. After crossing small bridge in valley veer left to go up steep bank heading just to right of Park Farm's farmhouse and buildings on skyline. Go through large wooden gate and turn right to go along short farm drive. Turn left onto roadway (no sign), the surface of which soon deteriorates. Pass barn on right and then pass Hollis Hill farmhouse (name not indicated) on left and buildings on right. Road surface has now improved. Now keep up steep, sunken road overhung with trees. Soon turn left **with very great care** to walk initially on the left-hand grass verge beside the very busy A44. Shortly, in the vicinity of minor road coming in from right, **cross the busy and dangerous A44 with very**

Monuments in Little Rollright Church

great care. Wait patiently for gap in traffic coming from both directions. Don't take risks. Don't try to cross as a group. You have been warned! Now continue along grass verge on right and soon turn right into the Greedy Goose's car park, thus completing Walk 17 **(A)**.

41

WALK 18

MORETON-IN-MARSH - BOURTON-ON-THE-HILL -
BATSFORD - MORETON-IN-MARSH

(A) Set out from the Redesdale Market Hall in the centre of **Moreton-in-Marsh** and walk approximately southwards, beside the High Street, which is also the Foss Way. Soon cross the Bourton Road with great care, with mini-roundabout to immediate left. Keep in same direction, beside the **Foss Way**. Leave shops behind and pass the University Farm Estate

> Start from - Car Park in High Street
> Moreton-in-Marsh,
> GL56 0AF
> See Gazetteer Section for Pub Details
> Length of walk: 7 miles
> Approximate time: 3½ hours

on right. Then turn right, off the Foss Way just before reaching the Inn on the Marsh, to go up Parkers Lane. (*We are now following* **The Monarch's Way**.) Pass pool on left-hand side of road and then pass Fire Station, also on left. Where Parkers Lane turns left, go straight ahead and almost immediately turn left onto wide surfaced path with backs of houses soon over to left. At end of surfaced path continue ahead on grassy path. At end of path go through large metal gate and bear right across right-hand side of field which may have caravans in it. In rIght-hand corner of field go through wooden kissing-gate and keep along right-hand edge of next field. Through large gap at end of field and turn right to go along right-hand edge of next field soon passing power-pole on right. Through large gap below oak tree and keep along right-hand edge of next field.

(B) Through gap at end of field with Upper Fields Farm visible to right and go along right-hand edge of next field. At end of field turn left in corner to follow curving hedgeline and soon turn right to go through large metal gate (*still on* **The Monarch's Way**). Go along left-hand edge of field with hedge to immediate left and through large wooden gate. (*At about this point we cross the infant River Evenlode, although it is not very apparent.*) Now go across field diagonally right (*leaving* **The Monarch's Way**) and aim for power pole. Bear right to pass waymark on short post and follow waymark's direction with wood now alongside on left. Near end of wood veer round to left and go through large wooden gate. Now veer right to go straight across field aiming to immediate left of barns (but it may be preferable to go along left-hand edge of field before

High Street, Moreton-in-Marsh

turning right onto track leading to left-hand side of barns). Go to immediate left of left-hand barn and go up short track and almost immediately through large wooden gate. Upper Rye Farm now visible over to right. Go along right-hand edge of field soon joining surfaced farm drive. Keep on this drive as it first curves to left in corner of field and then bears right to go through large

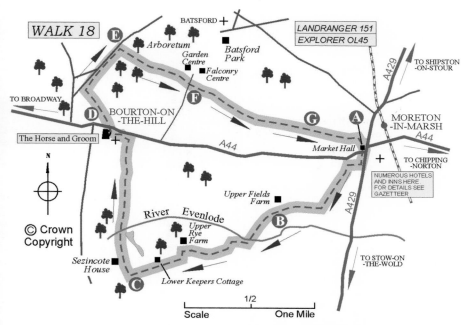

wooden gate. Keep on drive as it goes over cattle-grid (using gate to right of large gate). Now starting to climb up driveway and pass attractive Lower Keepers Cottage on right.

(C) Turn right, leaving farm drive immediately before cattle-grid and go through right-hand of two gates to follow path across field with fence to immediate left. (*We have joined* **The Heart of England Way**.) Pass large oak tree on right and start to drop down into valley. Good views of **Sezincote House** over to left. Lake visible over to right. At bottom of field through large wooden gate and over bridge crossing the infant River Evenlode, which rises on the hillside above to our left. This becomes one of the Cotswolds' loveliest rivers and flows into the Thames near Eynsham, north-west of Oxford. Immediately beyond bridge bear right through small wooden gate and go along path with wood to right and fence to left, beyond which is magnificent sloping parkland. Through small wooden gate and go up across parkland with fence to immediate left. At end of parkland go through two wooden kissing gates to cross narrow belt of trees. Go across field with fence to immediate right. Over stile beneath oak tree (*still on* **The Heart of England Way**). Bourton-on-the-Hill Church now visible ahead. At end of field go over stile and through large wooden gate. Now keep in same direction across field on well used pathway heading directly towards church. Through large wooden gate and up pathway with walls and houses on both sides, entering **Bourton-on-the-Hill**. Turn left with care to go steeply up beside minor public road. Church

Our approach to Bourton-on-the-Hill

43

now visible up to right. Pass Slatter's Cottage on left. Turn right at T-junction of minor roads and soon ---

Bourton-on-the-Hill

(**D**) --- turn left with **very great care** onto path beside the very busy A44 road. Pass the Horse and Groom Inn on left (*Tel: 01386 700 413 - Post Code: GL56 9AQ*) and after a few paces **cross the busy A44 with even greater care and with patience** to go up sunken surfaced track (signed below 30 mph sign - *Public Bridleway*). Soon go straight, not right and at top of track, with building visible ahead, turn very sharp left to go up partially surfaced track. Soon turn right (sign - *Bridleway*) to go through large metal gate. Keep up grassy pathway with hedge to right and fence to left. Keep in same direction passing wooded quarry remains on left. Veer slightly right to join track with sporadic fence to right. Through large metal gate and turn right **with care** onto public road. Ignore road coming in from left at inverted Y-junction and then start to pass large wood on right.

(**E**) Just before end of wood on right, turn right to go over stile and down, within wood with its boundary wall just to left. (*Now re-joining* **The Monarch's Way**.) Make a long descent - now within the **Batsford** Estate. Pass waymark posts and veer slightly left to join drive overhung with fine trees. Where drive bends to left by a cottage over to left, leave drive by going straight on following waymarks (*but keep left on drive if you wish to visit* **Batsford Arboretum**). Go down across large field aiming just to right of bottom, left-hand corner.

(**F**) Go through small wooden gate, veer right to cross surfaced drive **with care.** Now veer left to go through small wooden gate and go across field aiming for its left-hand corner (*still on* **The Monarch's Way**). Over minute wooden bridge and through wooden kissing gate. Keep in same direction across next field with parallel hedge and trees now well over to our left. Through partly-concealed wooden kissing gate in hedge about 30 paces to right of metal gate in left-hand corner of field. Keep along left-hand edge of next field with narrow belt of woodland soon to left. (*Route directions hardly necessary between here and point* **G**, *as route heads straight across a succession of fields. But they are included nevertheless!*) Cross small bridge, bear slightly right to go through wooden kissing gate and go straight across field to go between two oak trees following waymark direction. Through narrow gateway and keeping same direction across next field. Through wooden kissing gate beneath oak tree and keep in same direction across next field. Through wooden kissing-gate and keep in same direction across next field heading towards wide gap in cross-hedge. Through this gap and keep in same direction across next field.

(**G**) Through wooden kissing gate and go along left-hand side of next field, with football goal posts over to right. Soon turn left to go through wooden kissing gate and then turn right to keep along right-hand edge of field. Outskirts of **Moreton-in-Marsh** now visible ahead left. Veer left on to well-used pathway going towards houses. Go through metal kissing gate and down pathway with allotments beyond fence to left and tall hedge to right, into **Moreton-in-Marsh**. Cross public road with care and go down Corders Lane. At end of lane turn right into open area beside Moreton's High Street, the **Foss Way**. Arrive at the back of Moreton-in-Marsh's Redesdale Market Hall, thus completing Walk 18 (**A**).

WALK 19

SHIPSTON-ON-STOUR - ST DENNIS -
UPPER BRAILES - BARCHESTON -
SHIPSTON-ON-STOUR

Start from car park on the town side of the bridge across the Stour, Shipston-On-Stour, CV36 4AW
See Gazetteer Section for Pub Details
Length of walk: 7¾ miles
Approximate time: 4 hours

(A) Set out from car park on edge of **Shipston-on-Stour**, situated on left of B4035, the road towards Brailes. Turn left out of the car park onto B4035 and go over bridge crossing the River Stour. Immediately beyond bridge turn left to go down steep concrete steps. Bear right at foot of steps following **Shakespeare's Way** waymark and go along possibly overgrown path through bushy area with small trees. Eventually emerge from bushy area and head across very large field on well-defined path. At end of field go through small metal gate and turn right to follow well used path across corner of next field. Through wide gap in cross-hedge and go up track to immediate right of sewage works with reed bed. At end of track, turn left with care onto public road and go up its right-hand side to face oncoming traffic. Pass two entries to sewage works on left.

(B) Turn right at road junction by The Old Meadow House on left (*following sign - St Dennis*) and go along right-hand side of, a regrettably rather monotonous, road. We have now left **Shakespeare's Way**. Pleasant open views over to left. Go under high-voltage power-line. Go over small bridge in dip with good views over to right to **Brailes Hill** topped by its clump of trees. Ignore waymarked path to left and keep on road as it bends slightly to right. Pass Little St Dennis - house on left and dutch barn on right. Pass Autumn Cottage on left.

Our path beyond Point F

(C) Turn right at offset x-rds onto tarmac roadway (*sign - St Dennis Farm*) and soon veer right by St Dennis Farm on left. Pass partly-concealed barn on left. Keep on tarmac road with avenue of young trees and with open field to left and hedge to right. At end of field cross bridge over small stream by house on right and less evident one on left. Veer left over gravel driveways to go through large wooden gate possibly without waymark and veer further left to go diagonally across field aiming for easily-missed stile in cross-hedge to left of a notional line towards a high-voltage pylon in field beyond. Over stile and veer slightly to right of previous direction to go diagonally across next field. At end of field go through wide waymarked gap and keep in same direction across next field aiming just to left of barns ahead. At end of field go through right-hand edge of large gap and now aim to right-hand end of barns to cross narrower field. At end of field veer to left around the right-hand end of barns. Go

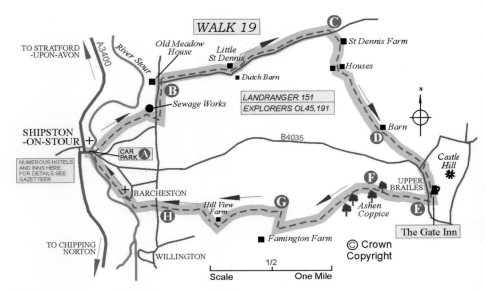

TO STRATFORD
-UPON-AVON

River Stour

Old Meadow
House

Little
St Dennis

C

St Dennis Farm

Houses

B

Sewage Works

Dutch Barn

LANDRANGER 151
EXPLORERS OL45,191

N

SHIPSTON
-ON-STOUR

B4035

Barn

D

CAR
PARK A

NUMEROUS HOTELS
AND INNS HERE.
FOR DETAILS SEE
GAZETTEER

Castle
Hill

BARCHESTON

F

UPPER
BRAILES

Hill View
Farm

G

Ashen
Coppice

E

H

The Gate Inn

TO CHIPPING
NORTON

Famington Farm

© Crown
Copyright

WILLINGTON

1/2

Scale

One Mile

across concrete hard-standing in front of barns before turning right to go along farm track.

(D) Where track bends to right by large willow tree on left, turn left through gap and immediately turn right to soon reach corner of field. Turn left in corner and head up right-hand side of field with hedge to immediate right. At top of field go through large metal gate and initially head in same direction up next field, but soon veering a little to the left to keep just to left of bushy hedge ahead. Good views opening up behind us. Veer slightly right at end of hedge to aim for stile in cross-fence ahead. Over stile and cross next field diagonally aiming for stile near right-hand end of fence ahead. Over stile and keep in same direction across next field aiming for stile in right-hand corner. Over stile and down narrow pathway between high fencing on both sides. Emerge to go across private driveway with house to right. Turn right onto public road at entry to **Upper Brailes** and almost immediately turn left by small green complete with Victorian horse-trough, to go along left-hand pavement beside wider road - the B4035.

(E) Pass The Gate Inn (*Tel: 01608 685 212 - Post Code OX15 5AX*) on left and soon turn right, off B4035, up Gillett's Lane, following sign - *Gillett's Hill* and *Ashen Coppice*. Go up steep surfaced lane which soon becomes rougher before going through large wooden gate. Keep in same direction passing house on right. Through metal kissing gate and veer very slightly right across small, rough field going up steeply before entering wooded area. Over stile in wooded area and keep in same direction going up steep steps which veer to right. Go up rough field following waymark, keeping straight up, and **not** forking right. Soon go through narrow belt of woodland and over stile into field. Keep across field following waymark's direction - this is the highest point on our walk. Good views in both directions.

(F) Through gap into Ashen Coppice and **down steep steps with great care**. Emerge from Ashen Coppice - splendid 180 degree views from here. Veer left to follow path down across field going between top two low-voltage power poles. On reaching grassy

46

track, this being the only dividing line between two fields, leave path and veer left to go along track. Keep to immediate right of wood and soon veer right to join surfaced farm track going parallel with edge of wood to left. Bear left at junction of tracks following bridleway waymark. Just before reaching metal gate turn right off track and through small wooden gate to follow another track initially round edge of hill. On reaching large tree bear right following bridleway waymark to go down across very large field aiming towards a group of buildings (this is Famington Farm). At end of field turn right onto grassy track and soon start to search for wide, possibly un-waymarked gap in hedge to left.

(G) Turn left to go through this gap and go down wide grassy ride with hedges on both sides and an 'avenue' of young trees. At end of ride turn right and almost immediately turn left to go through Bristol gate. Go down left-hand edge of field with hedge on immediate left and just before reaching corner turn left to go through small wooden gate. Immediately bear right to go down right-hand edge of field. In right-hand corner of field go over stile and keep along right-hand edge of next field. Over stile to right of large wooden gate and keep along right-hand edge of this next field with barns to right beyond hedge. Passing farmhouse, on right, beyond hedge and soon bear right onto well surfaced farm drive and go beside cattle-grid. Turn right, crossing entrance to Hill View Farm and go into field through small wooden gate. Keep along right-hand edge of field with hedge to immediate right. Turn left in corner of field and go down its right-hand edge, but well before reaching next corner turn right under a willow tree and go over stile. Now turn left to go down left-hand edge of very large field with hedge on left. Now gently dropping down towards the Stour Valley.

(H) On reaching willow trees to left, veer to left over rough grass in corner of field and **cross public road with care**. Go over stile and down left-hand side of field with hedge to immediate left. Near end of field turn right by stile on left to join more frequently-used path (part of **Shakespeare's Way**). At end of field go through large gap with possible metal gate and turn left onto public road at entry to **Barcheston** *(but go straight ahead and soon veer left across wide grass verge if you wish to visit church)*. Turn right and almost immediately leave end of public road to go onto track to left of churchyard. Veer right off track to go through wooden kissing gate. Initially keep straight ahead across field but soon veer left to follow path between trees to cross field diagonally. Through metal kissing gate in bushy hedge and keep in same direction across next field, following close to low-voltage power-line and parallel with the River Stour, over to our left. Through kissing gate below power-pole and small metal gate just beyond and keep in same direction across next field before veering slightly right to go parallel with

hedge to left. Through metal kissing gate and turn left to walk **with great care** beside public road (B4035) entering outskirts of **Shipston-on-Stour**. Immediately cross to right-hand side of road to use footpath beside it. Cross minor road coming in from right **with great care** and keep along footpath. Cross bridge over the River Stour and turn right into car park just beyond, thus completing Walk 19 **(A)**.

Barcheston Church

WALK 20

ETTINGTON - PILLERTON HERSEY -
PILLERTON PRIORS - FULREADY -
HALFORD - ETTINGTON

Start from - the vicinity of the White Horse Inn, Ettington CV37 7SU Tel: 01789 740 641 or the Chequers Inn, Ettington CV37 7SR Tel: 01789 740 387
Length of walk: 10 miles
Approximate time: 5 hours

(A) Set out either from the vicinity of **Ettington's** White Horse Inn or the Chequers Inn, on the opposite side of the A422 a few yards further on towards the south-eastern end of the village. Immediately beyond the Chequers Inn on left go to left, across its car park to go to far left hand corner of its garden to go through small wooden gate. Go straight ahead along left-hand side of field between garden fence on left and wooden fence on right. Go between metal gates to left and right and keep straight ahead over stile and small bridge across ditch beyond. Keep along left-hand edge of field with hedge on immediate left. *View of **Edge Hill** opening up to right.* At end of field go over sleeper bridge to go straight ahead through gap in hedge. Veer across field approximately 45 degrees right, aiming for gap in hedge below single oak tree. Over sleeper bridge in this gap and keep across next field in same direction, aiming for gateway or gap in left-hand corner.

(B) Through gap with possible metal gate and **with great care, cross the busy and very fast B4455 Foss Way**. Go down drive of Brick Kiln Stud Farm almost opposite, following possible bridleway waymark. Through electrically-controlled gates (OK dawn to dusk!) and keep to left-hand edge of gravelled driveway as quietly as possible as there are two houses over to right. Pass stables on right and then on left. Through metal gate and along track with trees on left and hedge on right. Soon through another metal gate into open field keeping along its left-hand edge with hedge on immediate left. Pleasant fields sloping up to right with two woods above them. Through metal gate to left of small willow-bordered pond. Keep along left-hand edge of next field, with attractive row of poplars visible ahead right.

(C) Through metal gate and turn right onto minor public road and after about 20 paces turn left off road to go through small metal gate beside large ones. Follow hopefully clear pathway initially keeping to right-hand edge of field but soon veering away first to left and then to right. Ignore cleared path forking to left. Through small metal gate at end of field and go along pleasant broad and gently meandering green road with hedges and young trees on both sides. This is known locally as *Greeny Lane*. At end of green road go quietly through farmyard of Coverwell Farm in same direction. Immediately beyond farmyard go through wooden gate and turn right onto minor public road. Follow road as it bends to left near the entry to **Pillerton Hersey**.

Pillerton Priors churchyard

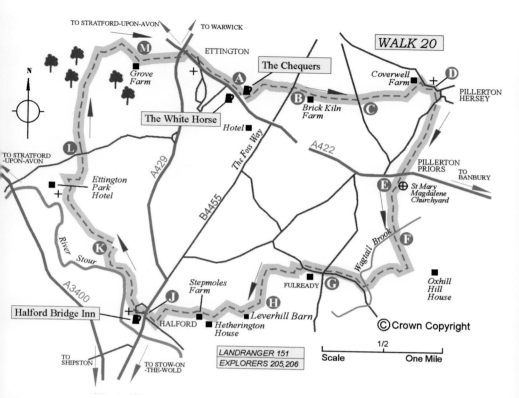

(D) Bear right by entrance gate to Pillerton Hersey's Church of St Mary the Virgin on left to go down public road for a few yards and immediately beyond the Old Vicarage turn right down grassy path between trim hedges. Pass small allotments on right and after a few paces ignore waymarked metal gate to right before veering left over small bridge crossing stream. Keep along grassy path with garden and house on left and fence on right. Go over public road **with great care** and go up slight bank and turn right to go along right-hand edge of field with old fuel tank and hedge on right. Soon turn left in corner of field and after 25 paces turn right to go through kissing gate. Go straight across field aiming for gate in cross-fence. Go through this small metal gate and veer slightly left to aim for top left-hand corner of field, first identified by tall ash tree. This tree is just short of our destination, so pass to right of it to aim for gate in hedge a few yards to right of field corner under a bushy hawthorn tree. *The field we have just come up across is a classic example of ridge and furrow. In some cases these are a survival of ancient field systems, but on clay soils such as here, this is more likely to be the result of ploughing to improve drainage.* Through this small metal gate in hedge and, after a few paces, through wooden gate at end of small spinney. Keep along top left-hand edge of sloping field with hedge on immediate left. Through small wooden gate in cross-fence. Through two more gates in cross hedges, eventually going between hedge on left and wooden fence on right. Keep to top, left-hand edge of sloping field. Through metal kissing gate and veer slightly left keeping to immediate left of cottage and house gardens at entry to **Pillerton Priors**. Through small wooden gate and still keep to immediate left of buildings.

(E) Over stile and **cross the fast and busy A422 with great care.** Go to immediate left of small triangular green and go up rough track soon passing St Mary Magdalene Churchyard on left. *This is still in use although there is no church here.* Beyond churchyard veer slightly right by the converted St Mary's Barn with its unusual glazed gable-end and then veer left with care into farmyard. Keep along left-hand edge of farmyard with wall to immediate left. Over stile and go through small

Barns at Fulready, just beyond Point G

spinney, which is part of St Mary's Barn garden. Over stile at end of spinney and keep in same direction across field with fence to immediate right. *The valley of the Wagtail Brook soon comes into view below us and well beyond is* **Brailes Hill**, *topped by its clump of trees; this lies due south of us at this point. On a clear day, the tower of Stow-on-the-Wold Church can be spotted (with binoculars and the eye of faith!), on the skyline ahead, well to the right of Brailes Hill.* Through Bristol gate (this is a small metal gate within a large metal gate) and veer very slightly left to go down large field aiming for gateway at bottom. Through another Bristol gate and keep in same direction across next field aiming for small tree in hedge ahead. Over bridge below small tree, crossing the Wagtail Brook. *This small stream rises on the hill slopes above Tysoe and flows into the Stour near Tredington.*

(F) After crossing the Wagtail Brook, veer right aiming for gate just to left of container immediately beyond fence. Go through this small metal gate and up field roughly parallel with track over to right, but gradually veering closer to it. Eventually go through small wooden gate on right and go up very rutted track keeping in almost the same line. At end of track turn right through small metal gate just before reaching large gate ahead. Now keep along left-hand edge of field with hedge to immediate left. Through large metal gate in cross-fence and keep in same direction before turning right in corner to go down field with fence now to immediate left. At bottom of field go through large metal gate and immediately turn left and go over wooden footbridge crossing deep ditch. Go straight up across field eventually joining track and then start to drop into small valley following track as it veers right. Through Bristol gate and over concrete bridge re-crossing the Wagtail Brook and go up track before turning right to walk with care along minor public road. *When on roads normally walk on the right-hand side to face oncoming traffic, but on any bend walk on its outer side to allow oncoming drivers to have as much advance warning of your presence as possible.*

(G) Over minor cross-roads (signed - *Fulready*) and then pass **Fulready** entry sign. Keep on road through this quiet hamlet, ignoring one waymarked track by gateway to left. Where road bends to right near end of hamlet, turn left over stile on right-hand bend beyond last house on left. Go straight across small field aiming for stile to immediate right of shed. Go over this stile, immediately veer half-left to go diagonally across narrow section of field, heading to immediate right of hedge-line pointing towards us. Now go through narrow gap in hedge marked by small waymark post, but not easily visible. Turn right beyond gap and go along right-hand edge of field with tall hedge and trees on immediate right and young woodland with deer fence to immediate left. *Good view of* **Tredington's** *church spire down to left*. Well beyond end of deer fence, at top, right-hand corner of field, turn left to go down field with hedge on immediate right. Ignore large gap to right with large barn visible through it across field and keep straight down `our` field with hedge still on right.

(H) After about 450 paces, reach clump of bushes projecting into field and turn right onto path through them (possibly not waymarked). Now veer slightly left to go along grassy path between two fenced plantations. At end of avenue turn right up track ignoring any waymarks pointing in other directions. Pass trees on left and keep on track passing to immediate right of wooden barn (*Leverhill Barn* - but not signed as such). Go round to the immediate right of barn on grassy track and keep on this through large gap before turning right to go up track along right-hand edge of field with hedge on right. At top of field, turn left keeping on track with hedge and trees on right. Impressive neo-Georgian house *(Hetherington House)* now visible ahead. Shortly before going onto better surface with large gate about 20 yards ahead, turn right onto narrower track. After about 15 paces fork left off track to go through wooden gate and then diagonally across field on possibly defined pathway. Pass barns well over to left and at end of field turn left through possibly small wooden gate onto track by small spinney on left. *Good view of* **Tredington** *church spire ahead.* After 60 paces turn right on to surfaced farm drive, joining **Shakespeare's Way** long-distance footpath, which we shall follow as far as Point **L**. Keep down drive as it drops slightly downwards (*Halford Church just visible ahead*) and after about 350 yards, well beyond road's lowest point and shortly before reaching gate across road, turn left to go through small wooden gate. Now go slightly left across rough pasture field aiming for kissing gate just to right of long bungalow. Through this gate, cross surfaced parking area and turn right onto estate road. Soon turn right again onto minor road into **Halford**. Pass bench on right but use path on left-hand side of road. Pass small bus shelter on right.

(J) Just beyond shelter, arrive at the very busy A429, **Foss Way**. *(Not far to the left, along the Foss Way, is a garage with a very useful shop and opposite it, The Halford Bridge Inn - Tel: 01789 748 217 - Post Code CV36 5BN.)* **Now cross Foss Way via traffic island with very great care** and veer slightly right. Now turn left down Queen's Street, pass phone box on right and go straight, not left, ignoring turn to Mill Lane. Use footpath on right of road but do not miss a visit to the church, which is on left as we bend to right. Keep on beside road, soon bending round to right by the Old Manor House on left. Shortly beyond the Old Manor House, turn left off road and go through large wooden gate marked *Henry's Meadow*. Keep in same direction as at our entry but soon veer down to the right in delightful miniature parkland. Through two small wooden gates and over small footbridge crossing small stream. Keep in same direction going straight up field aiming just to right of clump of trees. Through small wooden gate at end of thin wood, over narrow section of field and turn right to follow left-hand edge of field. It is not very visible but the River Stour is quite close to our left, below steep wooded banks. Keep on track with bushes to immediate left. Near end of track turn right and dip down to follow a much narrower track through overgrown area, probably boggy in winter. Now go up left-hand edge of this large field with fence and sporadic hedge to immediate left.

(K) Near top of slope turn left through small gap on left to go onto well-defined track leading between two tall oak trees. *Good views over to left of* **Newbold** *Church and beyond to Ilmington Hill, with Meon Hill to its right. One of the towers of Ettington Park Hotel just visible in trees ahead. Now cultivated, this land was all part of Ettington Park's parkland, hence the number of fine old trees.* Track now dips down into shallow valley before climbing up and gently bending to the right. Haha wall of Ettington Park's garden visible to left. Keep on track as it bends further to right and climbs steadily. Near top of slope pass woods on left and bend slightly to left. Turn right at open T-junction of tracks following waymark and keep on track with pine trees now on left. Veer left at Y-junction following waymark. Pine trees now on both sides.

(L) Through gap to left of wide metal gates and **go across public road with care**. Immediately go through gap to left of large metal gates following bridleway waymark (We have now left **Shakespeare's Way**). Go up rough track with small wood on left and hedge on right, but open field soon to left. Now track rises gently all the way and curving slightly round to right. *Stop from time to time to look back at the splendid views behind, taking in the spire of **Tredington** Church in the foreground and the long line of the*

Oxfordshire and Gloucestershire Cotswolds on the distant horizon, with the Burton Hills stretching away to their far left and Ilmington Hill, Meon Hill and Bredon to the far right. Pass two tall oak trees on right and almost immediately enter right-hand edge of wood. Very attractive woodlands now on our left. Woodland track levels out and becomes a wide but still-surfaced path for a short way, but then reverts to track. Track drops down for a short way and then starts to rise again as it emerges from woodland. Keep following grassy track with hedge to right and open field

Our track beyond Point L - fine views from here

now to left. *Good view to left of Meon Hill with Bredon Hill beyond, rising from the Avon Valley and looking rather like a great stranded whale.* Before reaching top of slope turn right through gate or gap just before meeting Boundary Covert wood on right. Go along left-hand edge of field with Boundary Covert wood on left. Through metal kissing gate and veer slightly left to follow track to immediate right of hedge ahead. *Fine eastward views now opening up including wooded Edge Hill and the line of the Oxfordshire Cotswolds to its right.* Phone mast now visible well over to left. Turn right at T-junction of tracks now heading for Grove Farm. Veer left through busy farmyard keeping to left of large grain silos and keep left passing old phone box on left and farmhouse on right.

(M) Now follow farm drive as it descends curvingly towards Ettington, with good views over to left. Where road bends to left, go straight ahead through narrow gap in hedge and over small sleeper bridge. Drop steeply down embankment, diagonally, left and **cross the very busy A429 with great care**. Now go left along right-hand verge and almost immediately turn right onto A422 at large roundabout (SP - *Upton House*). At first go carefully down right-hand verge of A422 immediately entering **Ettington** and passing tower of the second Ettington Church on left. **Now cross to other side of road with great care** and soon go over crossroads keeping on the A422 to go through Ettington. Ettington's third and present church up to right. Keep on path beside the busy A422. Pass Post Office Stores on left. Pass Ettington Primary School on left. Pass old Toll Gate Cottage on right and ignore footpath sign down to left. Soon arrive at the White Horse Inn on right and not far beyond, the Chequers Inn on left, thus completing Walk 20 (A).

ADLESTROP B-6 This modest village lies between parkland and a belt of trees climbing the hillside to its east. It has several pleasant houses in a cul-de-sac by the church. This stands in a well kept churchyard, but its interior has been over-restored and the only items of any real interest to visitors are various Leigh family monumental tablets. Their presence reminds us that Jane Austen used to come here often to visit her

Adlestrop

uncle, Theophilus Leigh, at his rectory, a partly 17th-century building now known as Adlestrop House. Theophilus, who was a member of the family who owned Adlestrop Park, was also Master of Balliol College, Oxford. He died in 1785.

The modest mansion of Adlestrop Park dates back to the 16th century, but its best feature is the south-west front designed in the Gothick style by Sanderson Miller, squire of **Radway** in neighbouring Warwickshire and a talented gentleman-architect in the best 18th-century tradition. Part of the surrounding parkland was laid out by Humphry Repton. There is a good walk northwards from Adlestrop, over the hill to **Chastleton**, following the **Macmillan Way**. Adlestrop is also on our **Walk 9**.

This village's name will always be remembered as the subject of Edward Thomas's highly evocative poem *Adlestrop*, the first two verses of which run:

> Yes, I remember Adlestrop ...
> The name, because one afternoon
> Of heat the express-train drew up there
> Unwontedly. It was late June.
>
> The steam hissed. Someone cleared his throat,
> No one left and no one came
> On the bare platform. What I saw
> Was Adlestrop ... only the name.

The station was closed many years ago, but the station sign and a station bench now stand in a small shelter in Adlestrop - a tribute to the young poet by the village he immortalised. Sadly Thomas died on active service at Arras in 1917, aged only 39.

ADMINGTON B-3 Lying below **Larkstoke** and the Ilmington Downs, this modest hamlet has only one outstanding feature - handsome 17th- and 18th-century Admington Hall.

ALDERMINSTER B-2 Astride the ever-busy A3400, this attractive village has wide grass verges which owe their existence to the old horse-drawn **Stratford and Moreton Tramway**. Alderminster's church has a stout 13th-century central tower and its impressive interior has several Norman features, many of which are the result of late-19th-century restoration. This church looks out over the River Stour to the little turreted church of **Whitchurch** standing some distance away in a circle of trees. The village's Bell Inn *(Tel: 01789 450 414)* is noted for its food and also has rooms.

Alderminster Church

ALKERTON D-3 This looks across the deep valley of the little Sor Brook, to its larger neighbour, **Shenington**. It has a number of attractive Hornton stone houses, all on steep slopes, with views westwards over the valley. Within the church, with its 13th-century tower, there is a real flavour of medieval times, with steps ascending from the nave to the chancel beneath the tower crossing. Do not overlook the fascinating carvings around the outside cornice to the south aisle, with men and dogs and at least one bear among the many figures. These are thought to be the work of a group of masons who also worked at Adderbury, Bloxham and Hanwell, villages all a little way to the east of our area. Alkerton's rectory was built by Thomas Lydyat, a 17th-century scholar and Fellow of New College, Oxford, who was tutor to Charles I's brother, Henry. When in Alkerton do not miss a visit to the delightful Brook Cottage Garden, which is on a hillside above the Sor Brook *(Tel: 01295 670 303 or 01295 670 590)*.

ALSCOT PARK B-2 Elegant early Gothick revival house in a well-wooded park on the banks of the River Stour. This was built in the mid-18th-century by James West, then Joint Secretary to the Treasury, and it appears that it was largely the work of father and son, Thomas and Edward Woodward, architects, builders and quarry owners of Chipping Campden, although two London craftsmen were also involved. It is also suspected that Sanderson Miller of **Radway** must have had some influence upon the design of the surrounding parkland (for more details read Jennifer Meir's *Sanderson Miller and his Landscapes* - published by Phillimore). The house is occupied by the West family and is not open to the public but there are pleasant views from the minor road leading from the A3400 to **Preston-on-Stour**.

Brook Cottage Garden, Alkerton

ARMSCOTE B-3 Attractive mellow stone village situated no more than three miles from the northern bastion of the Cotswolds, Windmill Hill, above **Ilmington**. It has a fine Jacobean manor house, very Cotswold in flavour, and several no less pleasing houses of the same period. Armscote has no church, but there is a hospitable inn in the centre of the village, the Fox and Goose *(Tel: 01608 682 293)*.

ASTON MAGNA A-5 Looking out over flat country that runs towards the valley of the Stour, this pleasant stone village is on sloping hillsides. It has a few pleasant houses and barns, and a little green, on which stand the base and lower part of a medieval cross. Overlooking the green is a church built in 1846 and now converted into a private dwelling. The circular earthworks to the south of the church are the remains of a medieval 'homestead moat', possibly connected with the Jordans, tenants of the Bishop of Worcester, and recorded as being here in 1182. Walk south-eastwards from Aston Magna, across fields and over the Foss Way, to the pleasant little hamlet of **Lower Lemington**.

ATHERSTONE-ON-STOUR A-2 With its Victorian church now in private hands there is little to see here apart from a compact mellow-brick Georgian rectory and some nearby offices and workshops. Atherstone is on our **Walk 6.**

BARCHESTON C-4 Minute hamlet just across the Stour from **Shipston**, with a manor house, rectory and church. The present manor house is largely 17th-century, but it was probably here in about 1560 that William Sheldon set up his tapestry-weaving enterprise, having first sent his man, Richard Hicks, to Flanders to learn the craft. The best-known productions from the Barcheston looms were the Sheldon Tapestry Maps, fascinating examples not only of tapestry, but also of the early cartographer's art. Several of these have survived, and good examples are to be seen at the York Museum and in Oxford's Bodleian Library. Stratford-upon-Avon's New Place Museum also has two delightful tapestry panels, with allegorical scenes. Barcheston Church has a 14th-century tower, and an interesting medieval interior, the contents of which include the lovely tomb of William Willington and his wife, carved in alabaster, and a brass to Richard Humphray - both from the 16th century. Walk south from here to **Willington** and **Cherington**, following **Shakespeare's Way**. Barcheston is also on our **Walk 19.**

BARTON-ON-THE-HEATH B-5 Quiet village on a small rise, with a tree-shaded green, on which stands a little 'well house', with an urn beneath a stone dome supported by three columns. This green is overlooked by handsome 17th-century Barton House, and beyond this lies a modest little Norman church, with small saddleback tower. Two sculptural details, one on the outside and one on the inside of a north chancel window, provide clues to

On the green at Barton-on-the-Heath

the possible presence of an earlier Anglo-Danish building. These were common in the north and east of England, but it is unusual to find one so far to the south-west. Other features of interest include an amusing fragment of Norman sculpture (a little pig running up the chancel arch), a small brass to Edmund Bury (1559) in the chancel floor, a 15th-century font, and pieces of beautiful medieval stained glass in the chancel's north windows.

BATSFORD A-5 A compact little estate-village at the gates of Batsford Park, a large 19th-century neo-Tudor mansion (1888-92), which can best be viewed from its arboretum (see below). Designed by Sir Ernest George, Batsford's building was supervised by the young architect Guy Dawber, who thereafter devoted his life to working in the Cotswolds, and who, by so doing, evolved his own 'Cotswold Style'. The church is slightly older than the house (1861-62), an ambitious neo-Norman building, with tall spire and apsidal chancel. It is worth visiting for the sake of the handsome wall monument to Thomas Edward Freeman (1808) by the sculptor Joseph Nollekins. Do not overlook the other monuments, to members of the Mitford family, the Lords Redesdale, the forebears of the fabled Mitford sisters, whose early years here, and at Asthall and Swinbrook in the Windrush valley, are so lovingly chronicled in Jessica Mitford's delightful book *Hons and Rebels*. However, for a fuller account of the Redesdales' life at Batsford and elsewhere, read Jonathan and Catherine Guinness's *The House of Mitford* or *Wait for Me*, the fascinating autobiography of Deborah Devonshire, the youngest of the sisters.

BATSFORD ARBORETUM A-5 Here are fifty acres of splendid woodlands, with scenic walks giving fine views eastwards out over the broad Evenlode Valley towards the Oxfordshire Cotswolds. There are over a thousand different species of trees, bamboos and shrubs, many from China, Japan, Nepal and North America, together with bronze statues brought from Japan by the formidable traveller and diplomat, Bertie Mitford, the 1st Lord Redesdale, and creator in the 1880s of this fine arboretum. Read all about Bertie and his descendants in the fascinating biography, *The House of Mitford* (see Batsford above). Plants may be purchased from a nursery by the car park and picnic area, and there is a tearoom *(Tel: 01386 701 441)*. Batsford is on our **Walks 7 and 18**.

BLACKWELL B-3 A delightful tucked-away hamlet with pleasant old farmhouses and cottages, but no special features of interest.

BLOCKLEY A-5 Built on the steep slopes of a hollow beneath the high wolds near the head of a small but prolific stream, this delightful village was owned by the bishops of Worcester in medieval times. It was Blockley's stream that provided the power required for no fewer than six silk mills, when the village was at the height of its prosperity in the early years of the 19th century. These mills provided much of the silk required by the ribbon manufacturers of Coventry, and at one time well over 500 people were employed here. See the old mill (now a private house) beyond the pool below the church.

Blockley Church

Still unspoilt by tourism, Blockley's little streets and terraces are full of character, with 17th- and 18th-century houses accompanied by dignified 19th-century buildings. Despite the prosperity of the village, the limitations of geography prevented the railway coming any closer than **Paxford**, but Blockley was not to be put off entirely, for there remains to this day an inn of character, still proudly entitled 'The Great Western Arms' *(Tel: 01386 700362)*. The nearby Crown Inn and Hotel *(Tel: 01386 700 245)* has open log fires and a warmly welcoming flavour. The church has a large airy interior, with plenty of plain glass and a flat ceiling. There is a Norman chancel, which was probably once vaulted, and a tower built as late as 1725, by local mason and quarry-owner Thomas Woodward, who appears to have copied certain features from the fine tower of his own parish church at **Chipping Campden**. Do not overlook the series of handsome monuments inside the church to various owners of nearby **Northwick Park**, at least two of which are by the celebrated 18th-century sculptor, J.M.Rysbrack, nor the two monumental brasses, both of priests - one in the chancel floor, and one (unusually) in the centre of the sedilia.

Street near the church at Blockley

The site of the medieval village of Upton is on the wolds above and well to the west of the village. Its presence was recorded in the Domesday Book and it has been excavated by archaeologists; but no trace of it now remains above ground. It was almost certainly depopulated in the 14th century on the orders of one of the Bishops of Worcester, who would have required it for profitable sheep-grazing. The Bishops were probably also responsible for the depopulation of three other medieval villages in the area - Dorn, Upper Ditchford and Lower Ditchford.

Explore the delights of Blockley on foot, and if possible walk to the south-western end, and up a track into Dovedale Woods, starting up a wooded valley known as The Warren and returning to Blockley via Norcombe Wood. Blockley is also at the start of our **Walk 7**.

BOURTON-ON-THE-HILL A-5 If only this village could be bypassed, all would be perfection. Even so, traffic rumbling up Bourton's steep and none too wide street does not entirely spoil this charming village. At the top of the hill stands the 18th-century stone-built inn with rooms, The Horse and Groom *(Tel: 01386 700 413)*, which has a wide reputation for good food. Then the road goes down past pretty little terraces of 17th- and 18th-century cottages, past the warm stone church, to the bottom of the village, which is here enriched by the elegant early-18th-century Bourton House, in the grounds of which stands a fine 16th-century barn (dated 1570). In 1598, the previous Bourton House was purchased by the parents of the unfortunate Sir Thomas Overbury, who was poisoned while a prisoner in the Tower of London, at the age of only thirty-two.

Bourton-on-the-Hill was once owned by the abbots of Westminster, who had great sheepruns on nearby Bourton Downs, and no doubt it was wealth from their wool sales that paid for the handsome 15th-century clerestory of the church. This feature together with the church's handsome three-stage tower gives it a totally Perpendicular look. However, within the pleasant cream-washed interior the massive arcade columns reveal its Norman origins - the pointed arches were probably a 12th- or 13th-century alteration. There are old stone floors and a minute 18th-century gallery near the north door. The beautiful bell-metal Winchester Bushel and Peck, dated 1816, are a rare survival of these English standard measures. A law dated 1587 specified that each parish had to have such measures, and they were used by local magistrates in the settlement of disputes (usually those relating to the payment of the hated tithes). Do not overlook the 15th-century octagonal font, nor the colourful 18th-century wall tablets. The lovely gardens of Bourton House are likely to be open at certain times. *For details phone 01386 700754.* Bourton-on-the-Hill is on our **Walk 18**.

BRAILES C-4 Upper and Lower Brailes make up a village of considerable size, strung out along the winding B4035, Shipston-Banbury road. In medieval times it was an important market town with the protection of a castle, the earthworks of which are clearly visible from the passing road and which may be visited on foot. In medieval times it was almost certainly the third largest town in Warwickshire, after Warwick and Coventry, and slight signs of many

The South Porch, Brailes Church

roads and buildings are visible from the air in fields adjoining the present main road. There are many pleasant old houses and also two attractive inns, both of which serve Hook Norton Ales, the 16th-century George Hotel *(Tel: 01608 685 223)* in Lower Brailes and The Gate Inn *(Tel: 01608 685 212)* in Upper Brailes. However the village is especially noted for the splendid Perpendicular-style tower of its Parish Church, known locally as *The Cathedral of the Feldon*, the Feldon being the pastoral area of

southern Warwickshire. Its lofty interior walls were scraped in 1879 and it has a rather cold feeling but the sheer size reminds the visitor of the long-vanished importance of Brailes. The village stands in delightful countryside beneath the shelter of **Brailes Hill**, itself topped by a clump of trees and an outstanding landmark visible from much of Shipston Country and the north-eastern Cotswolds. Our **Walk 16** starts from Lower Brailes and our **Walk 19** passes through Upper Brailes.

The Gate Inn, Upper Brailes

BRAILES HILL C-4 This is topped by a compact clump of trees and is an outstanding landmark visible from many places in Shipston Country. *"If we can see Brailes Hill, we must be nearly home"*, is a well-known saying in many Stour Valley families, including our own.

BROAD CAMPDEN A-4 Quieter and much smaller than neighbouring **Chipping Campden**, Broad Campden is tucked away in a small valley, with woods never far away - a delicious little village, well removed from the dangers of mass tourism, with

Stream beside the green, Broadwell

a warm little inn, the Baker's Arms *(Tel: 01386 840 515)*, and an outstandingly good guest house, the Malt House *(01386 841 334)*. It also has a series of delightful old houses, a small Victorian chapel and an 18th-century Friends' Meeting House with many of its original furnishings intact. Charles Ashbee (see **Chipping Campden**) converted a derelict Norman chapel into a house for himself soon after his arrival in the area in 1905.

BROADWELL B-6 Spread around a wide green, this pleasant village shelters beneath a hillside which rises up towards Stow-on-the-Wold. The green is overlooked by the hospitable Fox Inn *(Tel: 01451 870 909)*, which serves locally-brewed Donnington ales. There is a small ford at the village's lower end and not far beyond the green there is a handsome Georgian manor house and several 17th-century farmhouses. The church stands in a tree-shaded churchyard, with many beautiful 17th-century table tombs. It has an elegant Perpendicular-period tower, complete with reset Norman tympanum over its outer turret stair entrance. Do not miss the 17th-century monument showing Herbert Weston and his wife both kneeling at a prayer desk.

BURMINGTON C-4 An unassuming village above the Stour valley with a modest Victorian church in a well-mown churchyard backed by the manor house. The only items of interest are the Norman corbels which have been incorporated into the chancel arch. Not far away there is a fascinating brick and timber barn standing on staddle stones. Some years ago we talked in the churchyard here to an old man who told us that he was born in one of the cottages opposite and that he hoped to die there too. How humbling it was to encounter such contentment in our restless and ever-changing world.

BUTLERS MARSTON C-2 There is a wide green at the quiet end of this village on slopes above a small tributary stream flowing into the little river Dene. At the other end, closer to the road to Kineton, there is a path leading across a bridge to the parish church. This sits above a small valley in a pretty, flower-bedecked churchyard, with a Perpendicular-period west tower and a pleasantly mellowed Victorian flavour to the rest of the exterior. But once inside, the stout

Butlers Marston Churchyard

Norman arcading reveals the true age of this modest building. Here also is a medieval octagonal font, a good Jacobean pulpit and an early 20th-century alms box topped by a beautifully-carved hand.

CAMPDEN RAILWAY TUNNEL A-4 The best road between Chipping Campden and Hidcote Manor Garden passes a wooded embankment which was created by spoil from a tunnel excavated for the Oxford, Worcester and Wolverhampton Railway, built between 1845 and 1853. This tunnel was the site of the so-called 'Battle of Mickleton', when the great railway builder and engineer, Isambard Kingdom Brunel, led a gang of no fewer than two thousand navvies armed with picks, shovels and even pistols, in an ultimately successful attempt to oust the navvies of the original contractor, who had refused to leave the site. Read the full story of the battle, and of Brunel's fascinating career, in L.T.C. Rolt's outstanding biography of Brunel.

CENTENARY WAY A 100-mile circular long-distance path around the outer confines of Warwickshire and parts of it are to be found in Shipston Country. This was established to celebrate 100 years of Warwickshire County Council. Details will be found on www.warwickshire.gov.uk/paths and trails

CHARINGWORTH B-4 A quiet hamlet on hill slopes looking southwards over orchard country, with a fine early-Tudor manor house which is now a luxury hotel, Charingworth Manor (*Tel: 01386 593 555*). There is a pleasant open road northwards from here, around the Cotswolds' far northern edge below Windmill Hill, which then drops steeply down to **Ilmington**.

CHASTLETON AND CHASTLETON HOUSE B-6 Situated on the lower slopes of the Cotswolds, the high point of this small stone village is the splendid Stuart manor of Chastleton House. This has been sensitively restored by the National Trust and is well worth visiting (*Tel: 01608 674981*). It was built by Walter Jones, a prosperous Witney wool merchant who had purchased the estate from Robert Catesby in 1602. Possibly designed by Robert Smythson, the architect perhaps best known for his work on Hardwick Hall in Derbyshire, it has a fine five-gabled south front and a fascinating and highly atmospheric interior largely undisturbed by 18th- or 19th-century alteration. The most outstanding feature is the Long Gallery at the top of the house which has a beautifully ornamented and tunnel-vaulted ceiling. There is a topiary garden at the side of the house, an attractive 18th-century arched dovecot across

The South Front, Chastleton House

the road and medieval barns close by. While visiting here, ask to be told the story of Arthur Jones's plight after the Battle of Worcester, and how he was hidden from Roundhead troops by his enterprising wife Sarah, who spiked their wine flagons with laudanum, thus allowing the now desperate Arthur to escape.

The nearby church dates from the 12th century, although it was considerably enlarged about 200 years later. See especially the medieval floor tiles, the two interesting brasses and the wall tablets to two members of the Jones family.

Walk southwards to **Adlestrop** on the **Macmillan Way**, or south-eastwards to **Cornwell**, passing **Chastleton Barrow**. Chastleton is also on our **Walk 10**.

CHASTLETON BARROW C-6 A well-preserved, but thickly-wooded, circular late Bronze Age settlement. Unusually, its builders faced the encircling banks with large blocks of stone and some of these have survived. This may be approached by a bridleway from the road above **Chastleton**.

CHERINGTON C-4 Situated in the upper Stour valley between Brailes Hill and Stourton Hill, this attractive stone village has a handsome 17th-century manor house further enriched by a charming 18th-century Gothick porch. The largely 13th-century church is full of interest and has a well proportioned tower, fine Perpendicular-period windows, some with interesting medieval glass, a Jacobean altar table and rail and a delightful series of corbel figures beneath the roof beams. However Cherington's greatest treasure is the lovely 14th century canopied tomb chest topped with an effigy of a `civilian' whose name is unfortunately not known. There is a pleasant inn in this village - the Cherington Arms, which serves Hook Norton Ales *(Tel:01608 686 233)*. Cherington is on our **Walk 16**.

CHIPPING CAMPDEN A-4 *Chipping* was an Old English word meaning 'market', and Campden had a weekly market and no fewer than three annual fairs as early as the mid-13th century. In the 14th and 15th centuries it was without doubt the most important trading centre for wool in the north Cotswolds, and its name must have been familiar to wool merchants on the quays of Bruges and Antwerp, and most other cloth-trading ports of western Europe. William Grevel, described as 'the flower of the wool merchants of all England' on his memorial brass in the parish church, built Grevel's House in about 1380. With its splendid Perpendicular-style gabled, two-storeyed windows, this was to become one of the first of a very beautiful series of buildings in the honey-coloured local stone that were erected in the centuries that followed. Grevel's House is in private hands, as is the nearby Woolstaplers' Hall. The Tourist Information Centre is in the Old Police Station in the High Street *(Tel: 01386 841 206)*.

The lovely Market Hall was built in 1627 by Sir Baptist Hicks 'for the sale of cheese, butter and poultry'. He had made his money in the cloth trade, not in Chipping Campden, but in the southern Cotswolds and in London, for by this time Campden's wool trading prosperity had almost ceased, owing to the fact that since Edward III's time Flemish weavers had been encouraged to come to England, and wool was handled directly by clothiers in the Stroud valley and elsewhere, rather than by exporting merchants. Sir Baptist built himself the fine Campden House not far to the south of the church, but sadly this was later burnt down by Royalists during the Civil War. It was claimed that this was to prevent its falling into the hands of Cromwell's forces, but it appears more likely to have been set alight in a drunken spree by disgruntled soldiers before they were forced to flee. The only survivals are the lodges and gatehouse, and two pavilions and

The Market Hall, Chipping Campden

61

Chipping Campden Church

an almonry, the last three of which have now been restored by the Landmark Trust, and which, like all the properties in their care, are now available to rent by the week *(Tel: 01628 825925).* Just below the gatehouse and almost opposite the almshouses is the Court Barn Museum *(Tel: 01386 841 951),* which celebrates the skill and imagination of artists, designers, architects and craftsmen who have worked in Chipping Campden and the surrounding area. Its fascinating displays tell the story of the Arts and Crafts Movement from its origins in the early 20th century, up to the present day - more of this below.

Opposite the Court Barn Museum and just below the church is Sir Baptist Hicks's most enduring legacy, a row of delightful almshouses built by him in 1612. Sir Baptist became Baron Hicks and Viscount Campden in 1628 (the appointments no doubt arising from the substantial loans that he had recently made to his sovereign) but sadly he died only a year later. He and his wife are buried beneath a splendid marble monument in Campden's Parish Church. This is one of the great Cotswold wool churches, a fine Perpendicular style building with a handsome 15th-century pinnacled tower. Its interior is perhaps a little cold in feeling, but it contains a number of interesting monumental brasses, a series of monuments in the Noel Chapel, and an outstanding collection of medieval English embroidery, including a number of copes and altar hangings.

Chipping Campden's prosperity declined greatly in the 18th and 19th centuries, although local mason and quarry-owner, Thomas Woodward, left an enduring mark on the High Street, with the building of the elegantly classical Bedfont House in about 1745. However, Campden appears to have slept largely undisturbed by intrusions until the early years of the 20th century. Then in 1902 Charles Ashbee, a disciple of William Morris and Ruskin, moved his Guild and School of Handicraft from London's East End to Chipping Campden. This migration of fifty craftsmen and their families was a brave endeavour and full of idealism, but the Guild did not survive the rigours of economic depression, the First World War, and above all, the mutual suspicion that appears to have arisen between the Cockney craftsmen and the natives of Chipping Campden. However, Ashbee's ideals have in part survived, thanks largely to the artist and architect F.L.Griggs, who established the Campden Trust in 1929, and who did so much to preserve the Chipping Campden that we see today; thanks also to George Hart, the craftsman in metal, his son and grandson, who have kept the tradition of the Guild alive. The work of this remarkable family can be seen in the Old Silk Mill in Sheep Street, at the museum in the workshop originally established by Ashbee in 1902. Following on from this tradition of craftsmanship and design, the talented industrial designer, Robert Welch, established himself in Chipping Campden in the 1960s. Although he sadly died in 2000, his work and that of his family may still be seen at the Robert Welch Studio Shop in the High Street *(Tel: 01386 840 522)*.

Chipping Campden's present-day character still owes much to F.L.Griggs and his friends, and remains largely unspoilt. There are now far more tourist shops, restaurants and hotels than there were in Griggs's day, but there are still a few genuine country-town shops and small inns left. It therefore remains a pleasure to walk the length of the High Street, and up past the almshouses, to the splendidly-towered church, and on to the open land beyond, The Coneygree, which belongs to the National Trust. Before leaving this most attractive of Cotswold towns do not overlook the Ernest Wilson Memorial Garden, opened in memory of the great plant collector, who was born at Chipping Campden in 1876, and who made a series of expeditions to the Far East in the first thirty years of the 20th century. This delightful garden is situated in the lower half of the old Vicarage garden, and fronts on to Leysbourne, which runs northwards beyond the High Street.

Chipping Campden is the northern terminus of the Cotswold Way, the long-distance footpath which runs from here, following the approximate line of the Cotswold scarp, down to Bath, a distance of about a hundred miles. Why not walk the first few miles at least, up over the fields as far as **Dover's Hill**? Start by walking west, down the High Street, and turning right into Back Ends and Hoo Lane, and then follow the sign to the left marked 'Cotswold Way'.

The town's many hotels, inns and restaurants include the Lygon Arms *(Tel: 01386 841088)*, the Noel Arms *(Tel: 01386 840 317)*, the Kings Arms *(Tel: 01386 840 256)*, the Volunteer Inn *(Tel: 01386 840 688)*, the Red Lion Inn *(Tel: 01386 840 760)*, the Eight Bells Inn *(Tel: 01386 840 371)*, Joel's Restaurant *(Tel: 01386 840 598)*, Cotswold House Hotel and Restaurant *(Tel: 01386 840 256)*, Michael's Mediterranean Restaurant *(Tel: 01386 840 826,)* the Maharaja Indian Restaurant *(Tel: 01386 840 330)* and Caminetto (Italian restaurant) *(Tel: 01386 840934)*.

CHIPPING NORTON C-6 Lively little market town where the everyday lives of those who live and work there have so far not been overshadowed by tourism. It is built on west facing slopes, with the large Victorian Bliss Tweed Mill in the valley still looking less at home here than it would in some darker, deeper valley in West Yorkshire. It was in fact designed by George Woodhouse, an architect from Yorkshire's neighbour, Lancashire. Built in 1872, it closed only in 1980 and was then converted into flats.

The long Market Square or *Chepynge*, as it was called in medieval times (hence Chipping),is dominated by a handsome 19th-century Town Hall designed by George Repton, son of the better-known Humphry Repton, the landscape designer.

The Town Hall, Chipping Norton

The Square, which in the 19th century must have resounded to the horns of the twenty two coaches that were then passing through Chipping Norton each day, is also overlooked by pleasant 17th-, 18th- and 19th-century hotels, inns and shops. The town's Tourist Information Centre is in the Guildhall *(Tel: 01608 644 379)* and in New Street there is a small museum displaying items of local interest *(Tel: 01608 641 712)*.

The row of quaint, gabled houses was built in 1640 on Church Street, the cul-de-sac leading down to the parish church, which lies on slopes below. This fine, largely Perpendicular style building, no doubt funded largely with money amassed in the wool trade, has an unusual hexagonal porch with a vaulted ceiling. The church tower was rebuilt in 1825, but it is sad to recall that from its tall predecessor was hanged a brave but unfortunate cleric who, in the times following Henry VIII's break with the Church of Rome, obstinately refused to make use of Cranmer's English Prayer Book. The church's handsome interior was over-restored by the Victorians, but the tombs of Richard Croft and Thomas Rickardes, and the interesting series of brasses, make a visit here well worth while. To the immediate north of the church are the extensive motte and bailey earthworks of a 12th-century castle. Both features are visible from the course of **Shakespeare's Way** which passes through Chipping Norton.

The town's numerous hotels and inns include the Blue Boar *(Tel: 01608 643 525)*, the Chequers *(Tel: 01608 644 717)*, the Crown and Cushion Hotel *(Tel: 01608 642 533)*, the Fox Hotel *(Tel: 01608 642 658)*, the Kings Arms Hotel *(Tel: 01608 642 658)*, the Red Lion *(Tel: 01608 644 641)* and the Albion Inn *(Tel: 01608 642 860)*, the latter two of which serve Hook Norton Ales, or `Hooky'.

CLIFFORD CHAMBERS A-2 Situated not far from the Stour's confluence with the Avon, this delightful village has a single wide street bordered by wide, tree-shaded grass verges and ending at the gates of its manor house. This is of 17th-century origin but was largely rebuilt by the renowned architect, Sir Edwin Lutyens, soon after the end of the 14-18 War. Stone, mellow brickwork, half-timbering - all play their part in Clifford village and are enhanced by colourful gardens, many with a cottage flavour. The church has Norman origins but has a thin Perpendicular-period tower and a chancel that was over-restored by the Victorians. But do not overlook the pulpit, nor the communion rail which are both Jacobean, nor the two 15th-century brasses to Sir Henry Rainsford and his children. The attractive New Inn has rooms in addition to its restaurant *(Tel: 01789 293 402)*. Do try to walk beyond the manor house's entrance to go briefly alongside the watermill on the river Stour. Our **Walk 6** starts from Clifford Chambers and **Shakespeare's Way** passes through it.

The River Stour below the mill at Clifford Chambers

COMBROOK C-2 Beautifully sited in a deep wooded valley, the little village of Combrook stands below a grass-covered dam. This, we assume, was the work of Capability Brown who created two lakes in the valley as part of the landscaping of **Compton Verney,** the estate, in which the village then lay. There are a few old farmhouses and thatched cottages but many of the buildings were put up by the estate in the mid-19th-century, including a charming little Gothic-style church much ornamented with angels, a school and several estate cottages.

Combrook from its churchyard

But all is mellow in this quiet valley and the Victorian work does not offend the eye. Our **Walk 5** starts rom Combrook

COMPTON VERNEY ART GALLERY C-1 This is housed in a beautiful early-18th-century mansion, which was the home of the Verney family until the early 20th century. Thankfully it has been rescued from dereliction and sensitively restored by the Peter Moores Foundation and now houses a gallery of international standing. There are six permanent collections and a number of temporary exhibitions are also held here each year. There is a restaurant and an imaginatively-stocked shop. The mansion stands above a lake in a beautifully-wooded valley which was landscaped by Capability Brown and a visit here is well worthwhile. It is normally open from April until mid-December *(Tel: 01926 645 500).* Our **Walk 5** passes Compton Verney.

Compton Verney Art Gallery

COMPTON WYNYATES D-3 A beautiful, partly-moated Tudor mansion in a lovely setting below wooded hillsides. The unusual occurrence of brick in this predominantly stone countryside is probably accounted for by King Henry VIII's gift to Sir William Compton of the ruined castle of Fulbroke, near Warwick, and Sir William's subsequent use of the salvaged material for his new house. Royal visitors to Compton Wynyates included not only Henry VIII, but also Elizabeth I, James I and Charles I. This is a very private place and it is not easy to catch more than a glimpse from the nearby minor road.

On the skyline beyond the house there is a stone tower windmill, but sadly this lost its sails some years ago *(see illustration on next page).* It is possible to walk up to it by taking a path that starts from the end of a tree-lined track leading from the road well to the north-east of the house. On the skyline opposite, Compton Pike looks like the top of a spire peering over the edge of the hillside until it is encountered close by, when it is revealed as a sharp pyramid-like structure. Was it built to confuse and amuse, or was it the base of a beacon? Opinions on this are divided.

CORNWELL C-6 This delightful little village and its fine manor house were 'discovered' by a wealthy American lady in 1938 when they were both in a very run-down state. Realising the possibilities, she bought the whole estate and at once engaged the outstanding Welsh architect, Clough Williams-Ellis, to restore it for her. Williams-Ellis added several very personal touches which will remind visitors of his better-known work, the colourful, Italianate village of Portmeirion in North Wales. There is a small green with a village hall nearby, and a stream overlooked by cottages on slopes beyond. A short distance along the road to **Chipping Norton**, there is a glimpse through wrought-iron gates of the enchanting manor house, with its handsome 18th-century front concealing an earlier core. Between house and gates are beautiful terraced gardens which were also laid out by Clough Williams-Ellis when he restored the manor. Sadly the American lady's English husband was killed while serving in the Royal Air Force during the 39-45 War, and neither of them ever lived in the lovely house that they had brought back to life so imaginatively.

Compton Wynyates Windmill
(see previous page)

Cornwell's small church lies in parkland beyond the village and may be approached by a signposted path behind the manor. This low building has a central bell turret, and a pleasant but heavily restored interior. Do not overlook the font with its base made up of four carved lions. Cornwell is on our **Walk 17**.

CRIMSCOTE B-2 Situated just above the Stour water meadows this hamlet has just one feature of interest - an attractive old dovecote. This cannot be visited but is easily visible from the road.

DARLINGSCOTT B-3 A quiet village with several substantial farmhouses and a small Victorian church. There are fine views up towards the Cotswold Edge between Ilmington and Charingworth.

DAYLESFORD B-6 Minute estate village at the gates of Daylesford House, money from the owner of which must have paid for the building of the small but splendidly elaborate Victorian church. This was designed by J.L.Pearson, best known as the architect of Truro Cathedral. See especially Pearson's pretty tub-shaped pulpit, the brass to William Gardiner (1632) and the elegant monument outside the east window, simply inscribed 'Warren Hastings 1818'.

Born at nearby Churchill in 1732, Hastings had always hoped to buy back the family estate at Daylesford, and in 1787, four years after retiring from his controversial career as Governor of the East India Company's Bengal, he purchased Daylesford. Not anticipating the crippling expense of defending himself during his seven-year-long trial in the House of Lords, he soon set about building a fine mansion to the design of Samuel Pepys Cockerell, the architect to the East India Company, and later the architect of the better-known **Sezincote**. Unlike Sezincote, Daylesford is almost entirely classical in style, and only has a central dome in the Mogul style. It is surrounded by dense woodland, but in winter it is just visible from the public road a few yards south-east of Daylesford village. Daylesford is on our **Walk 9**.

DITCHEDGE LANE D-4   A green road in the vicinity of **Epwell** which forms the boundary between Oxfordshire and Warwickshire. This trackway may have been part of a prehistoric trade route, but it is more likely to be of Anglo-Saxon origin. Although there is now no ditch alongside it, there may once have been one marking the boundary between the two counties. the **Macmillan Way** follows this most attractive green road and there are fine, distant views from its ridge-route both to its left and right. It is reached most easily from **Traitors' Ford**. Ditchedge Lane is also on our **Walk 12**.

Ditchedge Lane

DONNINGTON A-6   There are fine views over the Evenlode Valley from this modest hamlet in the hills. It was here that Lord Astley, with 3000 Royalist troops, surrendered to the Parliamentarians on 21 March 1646, in the final defeat of the long and bitter Civil War. Sitting dejectedly amongst his captors at the end of the battle the weary Lord Astley was heard to say, '*Gentlemen, yee may now sit downe and play, for you have done all your worke, if you do not fall out among yourselves.*'

Donnington Brewery, although not open to visitors, must surely be Britain's most delectably-situated brewery. The accompanying lake, or mill pond, is the source of the little River Dikler, and its waters still turn a great mill-wheel. Donnington Brewery owns 15 inns, or `tied houses, and supplies many other free houses, all in and around the Cotswolds. It was brewing real ale long after the large breweries ceased to do so, and long before the Campaign for Real Ale forced many of them to resume. It is a truly Cotswold undertaking, with its inns always appearing to add to, rather than detract from, the charm of the towns and villages in which they are situated. If you appreciate

real ale, keep an eye open for Donnington's well-painted inn signs. Donnington inns in our area include the Black Bear at Moreton-in-Marsh, the Red Lion at Little Compton, the Fox at Broadwell, The Queen's Head at Stow-on-the-Wold, the Coach and Horses at Longborough and the Coach and Horses at neighbouring Ganborough. Further interesting and useful information, including details of all 15 inns owned by Donnington, will be found on www.donnington-brewery.com

Donnington Brewery

DOVER'S HILL **A-4** Here is a delightful crescent-shaped field-walk poised on the very edge of the Cotswold scarp. It was acquired by the National Trust in 1928, thanks to the efforts of Chipping Campden's F.L.Griggs, and to the generosity of that great historian, G.M.Trevelyan. There is a small car park here, and one can walk along the hillside, down to the edge of dense woodland below, or even back down to **Chipping Campden** on the Cotswold Way. On a clear day views out over the Avon Valley and the Midland Plain extend to Bredon, the Malverns, and the distant outlines of the Black Mountains and the Long Mynd. Identification of these distant hills is made easier and more interesting by a well-engraved viewing topograph not far beyond the car park.

Dover's Hill was the site of the famous *'Cotswold Olympicks'*, founded in 1612 by local lawyer Robert Dover with the approval of James I, the monarch having been approached through Dover's friend at Court, Endymion Porter, who lived at nearby Aston Subedge. These games, then held on the Thursday and Friday after Whit Sunday, included the usual horse racing, hare coursing, dancing and wrestling, but there were also two essentially local contests of a more violent nature: single-stick fighting, in which the contestants fought with one arm tied behind their backs, sometimes for hours at a time, with the sole intention of 'breaking the other's head'; and shin-kicking, the purpose of which was to reduce one's opponent to such agonies that he was forced to withdraw defeated. The more enthusiastic shin-kickers used to 'harden up' by beating their own shins with planks, or even in extreme cases, with hammers, in the weeks prior to the games.

Although temporarily suppressed during the Cromwellian period, the games were otherwise held regularly each year until the mid-19th century. By this time they had become the scene of considerable violence and drunkenness, a situation greatly worsened by the presence of Irish navvies, who were then building the nearby **Campden Railway Tunnel**, and they were discontinued in 1853, following an Act of Parliament enclosing the land. In 1951 the games were again revived, and since then they have been held each year on the Friday following the Spring Bank Holiday, followed on the Saturday by the *Scuttlebrook Wake*, a colourful fair which culminates in a torchlight procession from Dover's Hill back down into Chipping Campden.

DRAYCOTT **A-5** Lying in a broad valley overlooked by low wooded hills, this hamlet has an attractive row of cottages leading to a small 18th-century farmhouse. Walk southwards from here, up the fields to the road above **Batsford Park**, and then down again to **Blockley**.

EBRINGTON **A-4** A beautiful village overlooking a valley, through which the Knee Brook flows on its way to join the Stour above **Shipston-on-Stour**. *'Yubberton'*, as some of the older locals still call it, has many attractively thatched stone cottages lining its little sunken roads leading to the centre, which is itself overlooked by a war memorial and an unspoilt 17th-century inn, the handsomely signed Ebrington Arms *(Tel: 01386 593223)*, which also has rooms.

The church stands on a small ridge close to the largely 17th-century manor house, and above the rest of the village. It has a good solid tower and a Norman south doorway with a geometric design upon its

Cottages at Ebrington

68

tympanum, rather similar in style to the one at **Great Rollright**. Inside the church there are a few medieval bench-ends, a large, heavily-restored pulpit dated 1679, and a charming little medieval glass roundel illustrating the month of October - probably one of a series of twelve - with a jaunty peasant sowing grain. This feature is illustrated in the delightful book by Edith Brill and Peter Turner entitled *The Minor Pleasures of Cotswold*.

The whole interior of the church has been over-restored, but there are several fine monuments to members of the Keyte and Fortescue families. See especially the monument to Sir John Fortescue, who was Lord Chief Justice of England during some of the most troubled years of the Wars of the Roses. Despite a reversal of his fortunes after the defeat of the Lancastrians at Tewkesbury in 1471, he was allowed a gentle retirement at Ebrington until his death some years later, at the age of ninety. This was most unusual in an age when defeated enemies were generally despatched barbarously soon after the battle's end.

The two 17th-century Keyte monuments are equally interesting and we particularly like the notice reading, 'William Keyte Esq., A.D. 1632, left by will the milk of ten good and sufficient kine to the poor of Ebrington from May 10th - November 1st for ever'. It is sad to read a note below which indicates that 'This charge was redeemed 1952'; no doubt a practical step, but how dull! William Keyte's son, Sir John Keyte, must also have been a man of substance, as it is known that he raised a troop of horse 'at his own expense' for the loyal support of his sovereign, during the Civil War. Our **Walk 4** starts from Ebrington and it is also on our **Walk 3**.

EDGEHILL D-2 Small village just behind the scarp face from which it takes its name. There are two buildings of interest here - a thatched cottage and a `castle' - both are the work of Sanderson Miller, 18th-century squire of neighbouring **Radway** and are in the `Picturesque Gothick' style for which Miller was noted. The `castle' which is now the much-visited Castle Inn, serves Hook Norton ales and also has rooms *(Tel: 01295 670255)*. This was built on the point where Charles I's

Battlefield view - from the Castle Inn's garden

standard was raised on Sunday morning, the 23rd October in the year 1642 at the start of the first major battle of the Civil War. The Parliamentary forces under the Earl of Essex had come from the north and west and the Royalists from the south and east. On that fateful Sunday morning they were facing each other in the broad country that lies between Kineton and Edge Hill with the Parliamentarians based at **Kineton** and the Royalists on Edge Hill. Initially it appeared that the Royalist cavalry under the command of the king's nephew, Prince Rupert, had triumphed but lack of discipline led to much impetus being lost while Rupert's horsemen plundered the baggage trains of the Parliamentarian commanders in **Kineton**. So Edgehill's result was not as decisive as it might have been and although there were heavy casualties on both sides the two armies withdrew at the end of the day, both remaining as effective fighting forces.

The actual site of the battle is now largely in the hands of the military but there is a small monument beside the road leading from **Kineton** and good views over the country where the battle must have raged may be had from the lower edge of the woods that clad much of Edge Hill's slopes. These woods were originally planted by Sanderson Miller along the upper edge of his park at **Radway**. The doughty diarist, Celia Fiennes, coming to see Edge Hill in about 1690, `where was the famous battle in Cromwell's tyme'*, further remarks in her diary that, `the Ridge of hills runns a great length and so high that the land beneath it appears vastly distant ... tho' formidable to look down on it and turnes ones head round, the wind allwayes blows with great violence there'*. It is happily still very much the same today. Our **Walk 1** starts from Edgehill.

EPWELL D-4 A small Hornton stone village tucked away in a hollow not far behind the scarp face of the Oxfordshire Cotswolds, the top of which is followed here by an early trackway, known as **Ditchedge Lane,** which still forms the boundary between Oxfordshire and Warwickshire. There is a small ford just below a row of cottages, one of which used to be the Three Horseshoes Inn. The church has a small central tower, a thin Jacobean pulpit, and a pretty little Decorated-style piscina. The Chandlers' Arms *(Tel: 01295 780 747)* serves Hook Norton ales and is an unspoilt country pub where Aunt Sally can still be played. This is a form of skittles where players throw batons at a wooden skittle known as a doll. Epwell is on our **Walks 12 and 13**.

ETTINGTON C-2 Astride the A422, Stratford-Banbury road, this lively village has a busy shop and two inns, the Chequers *(Tel: 01789 740 387)* and The White Horse, which has rooms *(Tel: 01789 740 641)*. Ettington's original church lies some distance from the village, in the grounds of **Ettington Park** *(see below)*. This was replaced in 1803 by Ettington's second church, the remains of which are situated near the roundabout at the north-western end of the village. This had only a brief life span and was replaced by a third church, which was built only in 1902/3. It is of dark Banbury stone in a largely Perpendicular style and beyond the elevated chancel there is a fine east window depicting the Good Shepherd. Do not miss the interesting Tudor-period brasses of Thomas and Elizabeth Underhill mounted on a panel on the north wall of the nave, nor the elegant 18th-century wall monument to Margaret Underhill close by. Also tucked away in one

Ettington's second church

of the village's quiet streets, there is a delightful little late-17th-century Friends' Meeting House. Our **Walk 20** starts from Ettington.

ETTINGTON PARK B-2 Now a large country house hotel *(Tel: 0845 012 1888)*, Ettington Park was built between 1858 and 1862. It is without doubt one of the finest examples of the High Victorian style in the Midlands and, as such, is included in Simon Jenkins's book, `England's 1000 Best Houses`. The exterior is embellished with extravagant sculptural details, much of which illustrate events in the history of the family who built it - the Shirleys. It may, with permission, also be possible to visit the private chapel in the gardens of the hotel. This, the first of Ettington's churches, dates from about 1100 and was replaced by Ettington's second parish church in 1803 (*see previous page*). At this time the roof, east wall and north trapnsept were taken down, but the 12th-century tower has survived and the south transept has been made into a private memorial chapel for the Shirley family. This chapel contains a series of handsome Shirley memorials and has a particularly fine 20th-century stained-glass east window.

EVENLODE B-6 Lying in the broad valley of the River Evenlode, this scattered village has a Georgian rectory and several pleasant farmhouses, one with pretty Gothick windows. The attractive church lies on the western edge of the village in a churchyard containing several interesting 18th- and 19th-century tombs. It has a fine late Norman chancel arch with a mason's mark on its south side, a pleasing rood loft stair and a carved 15th-century pulpit.

FOSS WAY This Roman road runs diagonally across Shipston Country, through the towns of Moreton-in-Marsh and Stow-on-the-Wold, on its way between Lincoln and Exeter, a total distance of 182 miles. The permanent Roman occupation of Britain commenced in AD43, almost a hundred years after Julius Caesar's brief invasions in 55 and 54 BC, and within only four years the new Governor, Ostorius, had concluded its first stage by establishing his civil boundary along a line that was soon to become the fine road now known as the Foss Way. This then became a temporary frontier between the subjugated Iron Age tribes of the south and east, and their wilder, still unconquered counterparts in the more mountainous and less easily-controlled north and west. The Ordnance Survey, who are the arbiters in these matters, insist that Foss, without the e, is the correct spelling for this road. But when used within the spelling of various other place names, as in Stretton-on-Fosse, the e is added.

In the years that followed its construction, its purpose must have been largely military, with forts and marching camps established upon it at regular intervals (of which there is little visible evidence in the area covered by this guide), and with roads leading off it to the north and west carrying the legions towards the more troubled areas that lay beyond. It is one of the most direct of all Roman roads, and it is claimed that its course never diverges more than six miles from a theoretical straight line between Lincoln and Axminster in Devon. The best accounts of the Foss Way, and the other Roman roads in the area, the Ermin Way, the Ryknild Street and the White Way, are to be found in I.D.Margary's classic work, *Roman Roads in Britain*.

FULREADY C-3 Quiet hamlet in a broad valley through which the Wagtail Brook flows on its short journey to join the Stour near **Tredington**. There is a pleasant footpath from here across fields to **Halford** (*see Walk 20*).

GANBOROUGH A-6 Spread out along the A424, Stow-on-the-Wold to Broadway road, this sparse hamlet consists largely of a helpful Farm Shop and Pick-your-Own. This is close to Ganborough's Coach and Horses Inn *(Tel: 01451 830208)* which serves Donnington Ales and which has roaring log fires in winter and a large garden for the summer.

GREAT ROLLRIGHT D-5 Windy upland village just over the county boundary from Warwickshire into Oxfordshire, with fine views south out over a broad valley towards rolling hill country around **Chipping Norton**. There are no real features of interest here, apart from the Norman church. This has some grotesque gargoyles on its well-proportioned Perpendicular-period tower and a Norman doorway whose tympanum has a fish inserted amongst various geometric carvings. The porch in which it shelters is two-storeyed and its cornice is richly carved with an assortment of animals, flowers and the heads of men and women. Inside there is much evidence of over-zealous Victorian restoration, but do not overlook the brass to John Battersby, rector here until his death in 1522, nor the pleasant roof, with the names of the churchwardens in the year 1814 on one of its beams.

Walk north from here, down the scarp slope, across a valley, and beside a great wood, to the village of **Whichford**, or eastwards to delightful **Hook Norton**. If driving westwards from Great Rollright, possibly to the **Rollright Stones**, do not miss the splendid panoramic views, to both north and south of the road.

GREAT WOLFORD B-5   This village looks out towards neighbouring **Little Wolford**, across a valley through which the Nethercote Brook flows north to join the Stour, and so on to the Avon and Severn; but less than two miles away, streams flow south to join the Evenlode, which flows into the Thames. So, although the village stands less than four hundred feet above sea level, this is watershed country, and it was perhaps for reasons of strategy that a small Iron Age settlement was built here, the earthworks of which may be seen to the immediate south-east of the village. Wolford's medieval church was destroyed by fire in the early 19th century, and was replaced by a broad building, with a short chancel containing a number of monuments to the Ingram family. Its best feature is the tall spire, which is an outstanding landmark in this gentle south Warwickshire landscape.   There is an inn with rooms here - the Fox and Hounds *(Tel: 01608 674220)*.

HALFORD C-3   Although it is partly astride the Foss Way, this village has many attractive stone houses and cottages lining the small streets that branch off this busy main road. Just to the south of the village there is a lovely medieval bridge across the Stour that has been bypassed by a more modern structure. Stand awhile on the old bridge and gaze at the reed-bordered, willow-shaded river beyond. Up to the east of the new bridge is a fascinating early-19th-century octagonal house known as *The Folly*.

Halford's church of St Mary sits snugly in a small churchyard overlooked by many pleasant stone houses. It was heavily restored in the 19th century but contains several items of considerable interest. The tympanum over the north doorway is carved with the head of an angel with wings, probably Gabriel holding his message of the Annunciation; it is certainly the finest example of Norman carving in the area. On the right of the fine Norman chancel arch is a niche containing a defaced figure, possibly of the Virgin Mary. This was once matched by a

Halford's church tower

niche opposite, probably housing Gabriel making the Annunciation. See also the attractive font-cover, topped by carvings of five bishops' heads each with a mitre, and the single choir stall with its misericord depicting a strangely-distorted human figure. The Halford Bridge Inn has an archway indicating that it must once have given shelter to stagecoach travellers. It now provides both meals and accommodation *(Tel: 01789 748217)*. Our **Walk 20** passes through Halford.

HEART OF ENGLAND WAY   A 100-mile long-distance footpath between Cannock Chase in Staffordshire and Bourton-on-the-Water, near Stow-on-the-Wold. In our area it runs close to Mickleton, Chipping Campden, Blockley and Batsford. For further details see www.heartofenglandway.org

HIDCOTE BOYCE A-3   Here is a pleasant hamlet below the western slopes of high Ilmington Downs. It has a single, gently-sloping street bordered by flower-filled cottage gardens. Do try to look at the Millennium Monument beside the road at the lower entrance to the village.   Carved by a Ukrainian friend of someone living in the village, it shows an old man disappearing into a wall and a young man coming out of its other side. Some distance to the north of the village, the road from it is overlooked by Hidcote House, a delightful manor house which was built in 1663, probably by Francis Keyte of neighbouring **Ebrington**. This has attractively-curved gable-ends and mullioned windows. Our **Walk 8** passes through Hidcote Boyce.

HIDCOTE MANOR GARDEN AND HIDCOTE BARTRIM A-3   This was given to the National Trust in 1948 by the great horticulturist, Major Lawrence Johnston, who had, by that time, devoted forty years of his life to its creation. When he came to Hidcote in 1905 there was only the minute hamlet of Hidcote Bartrim and its 17th-century manor house, in company with only a single cedar tree, a clump of large beeches and a few walls.

The garden that we see today was therefore created from eleven acres of open Cotswold hill country. Major Johnston made not one garden but a series of small gardens (or `rooms'), separated by now mellowed walls and by hedges of hornbeam, yew, green and copper beech, box and holly. Amongst these magnificent hedges are to be found the Fuchsia Garden, the White Garden, the Bathing Pool Garden, and, in contrast to these formal creations, a wild garden beside a stream. These

In Hidcote Manor Garden

are enriched by grass walks and lawns, mellow brick gazebos and wrought-iron gates through which one can glimpse distant views of Bredon Hill and the Malverns, across the blue haze of the valley country through which the Avon and Severn flow. See also the Theatre Lawn, which is usually the scene for an open-air Shakespeare play at some time each summer, the Long Walk in the Kitchen Garden, which contains a fine collection of old French roses, the alley of lime trees, and the fine avenue of beech trees. The National Trust describe Hidcote as 'one of the most delightful gardens in England', and it would indeed be hard to dispute this claim. The Trust have one of their excellent gift shops here, and refreshments available include coffees, lunches and cream teas *(Tel: 01386 438333)*. Our **Walk 8** passes close to Hidcote Manor Garden.

HONINGTON C-3   Centred upon a wide, tree-shaded green, this village has a beautiful assortment of houses and cottages of timber, mellow brick or stone, merging together to produce a highly satisfying scene. Honington is approached from the A3400, Stratford to Shipston road, by a small road leading over a pretty five-arched bridge with balls upon its parapet. This is probably contemporary with the late-17th-century Honington Hall, an exceptionally handsome mellow brick mansion visible well over to the north, in parkland beside the River Stour. This was built in 1685 by a London merchant, Sir Henry Parker, and is enriched by a series of oval recesses between the upper and lower windows, in which busts of the twelve Caesars sit most comfortably. The house was lovingly restored in the mid-1970s, and incorporates a wealth of richly-contrived 18th-century plasterwork, especially in its entrance hall and octagonal Saloon. *Group visits may be arranged - Tel: 01608 661 434.*

Apart from its 13th-century tower, the adjoining church is contemporary with the house, and its elegantly-decorated interior reminds one of a Wren City church. It was also restored in the 1970s and contains several handsome monuments to members of the Parker and Townsend families. See especially the self-important but sumptuous monument to Sir Henry Parker and his son Hugh, a piece of work that typifies the spirit of the age in which they lived. In contrast, there are two monuments by the 19th-century sculptor Sir Richard Westmacott, less exciting, but also less worldly - the one to Lady Elizabeth Townsend depicting a mourning male figure by an urn - a typically poignant Westmacott treatment.

Thatch and stone at Honington

HOOK NORTON D-5   A large village situated in remote hill country that once yielded great quantities of ironstone. The old ironworks have long since vanished, but other evidence of Hook Norton's past importance as an ironstone centre may still be seen - a series of dramatic piers, the only remains of a massive railway viaduct that once spanned the broad valley to its east, carrying the long-vanished 'Banbury and Cheltenham Direct Railway'. There is also a Victorian brewery here (its red-brick fabric an unusual intrusion into the Cotswold scene) which still brews the most delectable Hook Norton Ale. This beer, like the village in which it is brewed, is known far and wide as 'Hooky', to all those who know a thing or two about real ale. Hook Norton Brewery owns over forty pubs, several of which are in our area. These include the Sun Inn *(Tel: 01608 737 570)*, the Pear Tree Inn *(Tel: 01608 737 482)* in Hook Norton itself and Gate Hangs High *(Tel: 01608 737 387)*, which is on a cross-roads about a mile to the north of it. Other Hooky pubs are indicated in these relevant town and village descriptions.

This village, with its orange-brown stone and thatched roofs, is well worth exploring. 'The Green' and 'East End' are both very pleasant, but we particularly favour the terrace in the centre of the village, with the Bell Inn *(Tel: 01608 737 432)* at one end and the church at the other. The latter is a large building of Norman origin with a finely-pinnacled Perpendicular-style tower and a spacious, pleasantly bare interior, the contents of which include a fascinating Norman font complete with sculptured figures of Adam and Eve, Sagittarius the Archer, and other signs of the Zodiac.

IDLICOTE C-3   Beautifully situated on a small hill, with a tree-shaded pool on its green and views eastwards over flat countryside to the dark outline of Edge Hill, Idlicote is little more than a hamlet, although it does have a small church. This has Norman origins, but its Norman doorway frames a Georgian door and this provides a foretaste of the interior, which is full of 18th-century flavour. There is a little west gallery, a three-decker pulpit and an ogival-shaped font cover, the later probably of 17th-century origin. There is also a pleasant 17th-century chapel with Tuscan columns dividing it from the chancel. Nearby Idlicote House is a dignified early-19th-century building, while close by there is a fine 18th-century dovecote, which once provided shelter for no fewer than 1002 nesting birds.

Tree-shaded pool at Idlicote

ILMINGTON B-3   A delightful stone village lying beneath Windmill Hill, northerly bastion of the Cotswolds, and still very 'Cotswold' in flavour. It spreads itself comfortably below the hill slopes, and to be properly savoured should be explored on foot. Here will be found a wealth of old houses and cottages, many beside small paths which stray away from the road that encircles the village. There is a lovingly-restored manor house, the beautiful gardens of which are normally open to the public at least twice a year. There are also two very pleasant inns, the Howard Arms *(Tel: 01608 682 226)* with a wide reputation for good food, and the Red Lion *(Tel: 01608 682 366)*, which is very popular with walkers, and which serves Hook Norton Ales.

The quietly-sited church overlooks two pools in a field in the very heart of the village. It is a largely Norman building, with Norman north and south doorways and chancel arch, and Norman windows in the aisle. Once beyond the 16th-century porch, one comes upon splendid oak pews and other furnishings. These were all installed in the 1930s, and were the work of master-craftsman, Robert Thompson, whose descendants still produce their stout oak furniture in his original workshops in the little village of Kilburn, beneath the steep slopes of the far-off North York Moors. All of Robert Thompson's work, and that of his descendants too, includes a unique signature, an individually carved mouse. Can you find the eleven mice that he carved upon the Ilmington oak? However, during your search for the mice, do not overlook the severely classical monument to Francis Canning and his wife by the early 19th-century sculptor, Sir Richard Westmacott, other examples of whose work will be found at **Honington** and **Preston-on-Stour**. Westmacott, much in the spirit of his times, was very fond of weeping figures and classical urns, and these features will be found in all three of the village churches concerned. The unusual lantern-like structure by the south porch is an early-19th-century monument to members of the Sansom family.

Our **Walk 2** starts from Ilmington. There is also a pleasantly quiet road running south from Ilmington, along the eastern slopes of Windmill Hill to **Charingworth**, with fine views over the Vale of Red Horse to the distant line of **Edge Hill**.

KIFTSGATE COURT GARDEN A-3 *(Tel: 01386 438777)*   This is perhaps not as well-known as neighbouring **Hidcote Manor Garden**, but it should on no account be missed. Kiftsgate Court, situated on the very edge of the Cotswold scarp above Mickleton, is a largely Victorian house, with an 18th-century portico which was moved piece by piece up from Mickleton Manor on a specially-constructed light railway. Most of the garden was created in the years following the First World War, by Mrs Heather Muir, and she was no doubt helped and inspired by her neighbour and

75

friend, Major Johnston, the creator of nearby **Hidcote Manor Garden**. Kiftsgate Garden's steep hillside setting is more dramatic than Hidcote's, and Mrs Muir took full advantage of this in her splendid design.

Mrs Muir's daughter and granddaughter, Mrs Binny and Mrs Chambers, have carried on the Kiftsgate tradition, and today the garden continues to evolve. There are paths, flower-beds, shrubs and trees on the terraced

A hint of the Mediterranean at Kiftsgate Court Garden

areas above the scarp, and a steep cliff with pine-trees, and winding paths leading to a swimming pool on a grassy terrace at its foot, with views down a wooded combe to the Vale of Evesham. Come here in summertime, when the air is heavy with the scent of roses, and the blue swimming pool, viewed through the pine-trees from the steep hillside above, brings a hint of the Mediterranean to this lovely garden enfolded in the Cotswold hills. Teas are available here. Walk up to Kiftsgate from **Mickleton** using our **Walk 8**.

KINETON D-2 First mentioned in a Saxon charter of AD 969, the large village of Kineton was for several centuries a market town of some importance. However its market square is now a quiet backwater. The earthworks of a medieval castle, known as King John's Castle, overlook a small bend in the little River Dene, but there is no proven connection with the monarch in question. There is much modern building on Kineton's fringes, but in addition to the 17th- and 18th-century houses lining the tranquil Market Square, there are several pleasant houses of the same period in Bridge Street. Kineton has two lively inns, the Swan Hotel *(Tel: 01926 640 876)*, which has its own skittle alley, and the Carpenters' Arms *(Tel: 01926 640 364)*. It also has a restaurant, Shukurs Brasserie *(Tel: 01926 642 171)* and several very useful and friendly shops.

The solid Hornton stone church tower was completed in about 1315, but the rest is largely 19th-century work. It is sad to note that the work carried out in the mid-18th century by Sanderson Miller, squire of neighbouring **Radway**, was amongst that replaced by Victorian enthusiasts. However the interior of the church was treated with rather more sympathy than we might have hoped for, and the Victorian architect concerned left the stone-flagged floors undisturbed and did not scrape the walls down to reveal stark over-pointed stonework, as is so often the case with 19th-century restoration. Do not overlook the fine round-topped churchwardens' chest nor the handsome 18th-century monuments in the chancel.

During the battle of **Edgehill** in 1642, the baggage train of the Parliamentarian generals was quartered at Kineton, and much blood was spilt here, first when Prince Rupert's cavalry broke through into the village during the battle and two days later, when Rupert again fell upon the remnants of the Parliamentary force, their wounded and their sick, `and several wagons loaded with muskets and pikes, and all sorts of ammunition'. These events appear to have struck terror into the inhabitants of this normally tranquil village, and within a few months there were reports of supernatural happenings in Kineton and the surrounding countryside ... reports of such substance that sensational pamphlets were published, thereby prompting the King to send a party of officers from his headquarters at Oxford to investigate their claims. For many years since there was talk in Kineton of wild cries and great commotion on each night of 23rd October, the anniversary of the battle; but today all now appears to be quiet.

LARKSTOKE AND ILMINGTON DOWNS A-3

At 850 feet above sea level, this is the highest point in Warwickshire, and one of the northern bastions of the Cotswolds. Despite the presence of a small TV transmitting station, this is still reasonably good walking country, and there are fine open views northwards out over the Avon valley, and eastwards to the wooded silhouette of **Edge Hill** and the rolling Northamptonshire uplands that lie beyond. *Lark*

Quiet road down from Larkstoke

Stoke received a separate entry in the Domesday Book of 1086, but there is now no trace of any ancient village on these windy hillsides, nor in the woodlands below. Larkstoke is on our **Walks 2 and 8**.

LITTLE COMPTON C-5

Situated in a sheltered hollow between Barton Hill and the main Cotswold Edge, this pleasant village, Warwickshire's southernmost, is over the watershed into the 'land of the Thames'. This great river may seem very far away, but the stream on which Little Compton lies flows west to join the Evenlode below **Moreton-in-Marsh**, where this tributary river is itself near the start of its quiet journey to join the Thames just above Oxford. The little church retains its 14th-century tower with saddleback roof, but the rest of the building dates from the 1860s, and is not of great interest to visitors. In the churchyard there is a gravestone carved by one of the 20th century's outstanding sculptors, Eric Gill; a simple but fine example of his craft. The lovely 17th-century manor house next to the church was the home of Bishop Juxon, who had the unenviable task of attending Charles I at his trial and subsequent execution on the scaffold outside the Banqueting Hall, Whitehall. During their walk to this place of execution, Juxon was observed by the king to be weeping, and the king is supposed to have exclaimed, 'Leave all this my Lord; we have no time for it.' This terse comment appears at least to have stopped Juxon's tears, and after some years he received substantial consolation, for when his monarch's son, Charles II, was finally crowned in 1660, he was appointed Archbishop of Canterbury - a post he held until his death, sadly only three years later.

If you pass through Little Compton during 'opening hours', call at the Red Lion Inn *(Tel: 01608 674 397)*. This cheerful pub serves Donnington Ale - real ale which is brewed at the delectable little **Donnington Brewery**, a short distance to the north of Stow-on-the-Wold. The Red Lion also provides Bed and Breakfast. Our **Walk 10** starts from here.

LITTLE ROLLRIGHT C-6

Here, in a quiet setting beneath the hills, are a fine 17th-century manor house, a modest rectory of the same period, a few cottages, and a delightful little church. This is a largely Perpendicular-style building, but its squat tower and south window date from the 17th century. It has a simple interior, with pleasant Perpendicular-period windows and two gorgeous 17th-century monuments - canopied tomb chests to members of the Dixon family. These tombs make it clear that the Dixons must have been persons of considerable substance, probably sheep graziers. Please, do not miss a visit to this very satisfying little building. It can be visited by walkers on **Shakespeare's Way**, which passes by the edge of this minute village. Little Rollright is also on our **Walk 17**.

LITTLE WOLFORD C-5 A hamlet of Victorian estate cottages and unexciting 20th-century houses, situated in gently undulating countryside, with views towards the spires of **Todenham** and **Great Wolford**, out over the valley through which the little Nethercote Brook flows, on its way to join the Stour a mile or so to the north. Any dullness is relieved by tantalising glimpses of Little Wolford's fine Tudor manor house. This is in a pleasing blend of stone and timber-framing - appropriate in an area which lies between the ancient forest country of Warwickshire and the bare stone uplands of the Oxfordshire Cotswolds.

LONGBOROUGH A-6 Attractively-sited village on a hill slope looking eastwards over the broad Evenlode Valley, with a pleasant inn called the Coach and Horses *(Tel: 01451 830 325)* which serves locally-brewed Donnington Ales. There are also many neat houses and cottages and a church with Norman origins which once belonged to Hailes Abbey. It has a 13th-century tower with an added upper stage with pinnacles and gargoyles in the best Perpendicular tradition. The sunken path to the south porch is overlooked by the beautiful Decorated-style windows of the 14th-century south transept. This houses the very grand 17th-century monument to Sir William Leigh, complete with his wife and children, and a monument to a 14th-century knight and his lady, for whom this transept was probably built. The north transept, added after the demolition of nearby **Sezincote** church, is sealed off and houses the tomb of Sir Charles Cockerell, the builder of Sezincote. This church contains several other items of interest, but do make a point of looking at the beautiful 14th-century font - a tall richly-sculptured piece.

This village is also noted for its Longborough Festival Opera, held annually in June and July. With its dramatic front, Longborough's opera house has no fewer than 500 seats and an orchestra pit for 65 players. For further details see www.lfo.org.uk

LONG COMPTON C-5 This stone village stretches out along the A3400 for over half a mile, to the very foot of the long road that climbs up over the Cotswold Edge, across the county boundary from Warwickshire into Oxfordshire. There is considerable modern building at its northern end, and the main road is always busy with traffic; but despite this Long Compton has much to offer. It has a first-rate inn, with rooms, the Red Lion *(Tel: 01608 684 968)*, many trim houses and cottages, and a church whose handsome Perpendicular-period tower looks westwards over a large bumpy field which must have been the site of the original village. The church's lovely south porch is approached by a yew-lined path leading from a delightful little two-storeyed lych gate. This was once a small timber-framed cottage, the lower storey of which has been removed. The core of the church is 13th-century, but externally it appears to be almost entirely Perpendicular. See the nave roof, the charming little Perpendicular style south aisle

Unusual lych gate at Long Compton

78

chapel, and in the porch the pathetically-worn effigy of a lady. For a full account of life at Long Compton and in the countryside that surrounds it, read Edward Rainsberry's delightful book, *Through the Lych Gate*, published by the Roundwood Press, which is unfortunately long out of print.

Do not overlook the interesting Millennium Chronolog, beside the main road and almost opposite the Village Hall.

LOWER LEMINGTON B-5 This is now no more than a quiet little hamlet with a farm, a few houses and a small church - all spread around an open field-cum-farmyard. But the undulating fields surrounding it conceal the remains of a larger medieval village, and on the road to its south there is a substantial 16th- and 17th-century manor house. The little church in its stone-walled churchyard has a small bellcote where the nave roof meets that of the chancel, and a narrow Norman doorway within its porch. The chancel was damaged during the Civil War, but the exceptionally narrow Norman chancel arch, with minute squints on either side, has survived. There are pleasant old Commandment Boards, an early Norman tub font, an 18th-century two-decker pulpit and a small 17th-century brass to two brothers, Charles and Peter Greville.

MACMILLAN WAY, THE
A 290-mile coast-to-coast footpath linking Boston on the shore of the North Sea with Abbotsbury on the Dorset coast. It enters the area covered by this book in the vicinity of **Edge Hill** and leaves it near **Oddington**. Apart from providing a fine opportunity to journey across England or at least to walk across some of the best of Shipston Country, its other aim is to raise funds for Macmillan Cancer Support. For further

On the course of the Macmillan Way just beyond Sunrising Hill

information see www.macmillanway.org   See also **Shakespeare's Way,** another long-distance path that traverses Shipston Country, and also **Whichford Wood**, where the two paths converge.

MAUGERSBURY A-6 Quiet hamlet on the south-eastern slopes of Stow-on-the-Wold's hill, with pleasant views across to Icomb Hill. There are several pleasant farmhouses, but no features of special interest apart from St Edward's Well. This is situated in an overgrown late-18th-century garden (on private ground) on both sides of the road between the village and the **Foss Way**, and is connected by a tunnel under the road. It is not certain with which St Edward the well is supposed to be connected - Edward, King and Martyr, Edward the Confessor, or Edward the Hermit - the latter being a shadowy local figure from early Christian times. The same mystery surrounds this 'St Edward connection' at nearby **Stow-on-the-Wold**.

MICKLETON A-3 This busy, almost town-like, village has considerable modern development on its fringes, and is rather disturbed by traffic on the busy B4632. However, it lies in attractive surroundings immediately beneath the Cotswold Edge, and has several attractive stone houses and cottages in addition to those of thatch and half-timber. The little Victorian Memorial Fountain close by the Three Ways Hotel is an attractive feature - an unusually restrained piece of work by William Burges, the architect of Cardiff Castle and Castle Coch, two supreme examples of the High Victorian Gothic style. The Three Ways Hotel (*Tel: 01386 438 429*) is noted for its Pudding Club. Mickleton's other inn is the nearby King's Arms (*Tel: 01386 438 257*) and both establishments have a reputation for good food.

Turn up beside handsome 'Cotswold-Queen Anne' style-Medford House, to visit the church, which lies on the southern edge of the village, with pleasant views up towards the wooded Cotswold Edge. This church has a fine 14th-century tower and spire, and a most unusual 17th-century two-storeyed porch. Inside will be found a 12th-century crucifix or rood (over the north aisle chapel altar), some stout, late Norman arcading, and a monument to the 18th-century architect, builder and quarry-owner, Thomas Woodward of **Chipping Campden**, erected by his grandson, Edward. There is considerable evidence of Victorian restoration in the shape of the east window and most of the woodwork, but Mickleton Church has retained an atmosphere that makes a visit here well worth while.

Our **Walk 8** starts from Mickleton.

MONARCH'S WAY, THE A 615-mile long-distance path based on the route taken by Charles II during his escape after the Battle of Worcester in 1651. It runs from Worcester to Shoreham on the Sussex coast and passes through the western fringes of Shipston Country. For more details see www.ldwa.org.uk

MORETON-IN-MARSH B-5 The intrepid late-17th-century traveller and diarist, Celia Fiennes, visited Moreton several times, as she had a widowed aunt living there. Her succinct description of '*Morton Hindmost*' as '*a little neate stone built town, good Innes for traveller*' could hardly be bettered today. As Mistress Celia pointed out, it lay on the main route from London and Oxford to the cities of Worcester and Hereford, and the centre of Wales; and this probably accounted even more strongly for Moreton's prosperity than did its position astride the **Foss Way**.

It appears that this '*little neate stone built town*' was also once called Moreton Henmarsh, the Henmarsh being low-lying country much frequented by coots and moorhens; but we still find Celia's 'Morton Hindmost' a more endearing name. The origins of the town are rather obscure, but the oldest part grew up around the church, a former chapel of ease for nearby **Bourton-on-the-Hill**.

Moreton's Market Hall

The present parish church, lying to the east of the High Street, and south of Oxford Street, is almost entirely Victorian, and is not of great interest to visitors. However, the elegant 18th-century house to its immediate east should not be overlooked.

Almost all of Moreton-in-Marsh's interesting features are situated on its High Street, with a series of stonebuilt shops, houses and coaching inns facing each other across the broad Foss Way, but divided by busy traffic passing along it between the Midlands and the South-West. The Manor House Hotel *(Tel: 01608 650 501)* and the Redesdale Arms *(Tel: 01608 650 308)* are both pleasing buildings, and the White Hart Royal Hotel *(Tel: 01608 650731)* claims the distinction of having provided shelter for Charles I - on 2nd July 1644. Moreton's numerous pubs include the Inn on the Marsh *(Tel: 01608 650 709)*, the Black Bear *(Tel: 01608 650 501)* and the Wellington Inn *(Tel: 01608 650 936)*, which serves Hook Norton Ales. *For details of other hotels, inns and B&Bs see* *www.cotswolds.info/accommodation/moreton-in-marsh-lodgings* .

The little 16th-century Curfew Tower on the corner of Oxford Street has a bell dated 1633, and this used to be rung each evening until as recently as 1860. On the other side of the High Street is the town's dominant feature, the confidently neo-Tudor Redesdale Market Hall, built in 1887 to the designs of Sir Ernest George, who was soon to carry out a similar commission for Lord Redesdale - the design of the 'Cotswold-Elizabethan' mansion, at nearby **Batsford Park**.

The coming to Moreton in 1843 of Brunel's Oxford, Worcester and Wolverhampton Railway brought a connection with the outside world that some of Moreton's neighbours must have envied at the time, and a certain robust quality appears to have survived here to this day (see also the **Stratford and Moreton Tramway**). So despite the traffic, do take time off to walk down both sides of Moreton's long High Street - there are several interesting and attractive shops, and the tree-lined greens at the northern end are especially pleasing.

NEWBOLD-ON-STOUR B-3 Most of this village is strung out along the A3400 although it has a wide village green just to the west of this busy main road. It has two lively inns, the White Hart (Tel: *01789 450 205)* and the Bird in Hand *(Tel: 01789 450 253)*, the latter of which serves Hook Norton Ales, or `Hooky'. The church was built as recently as 1835 and is a simple building of local stone with a nave and chancel. It once had a spire but this had to be removed in 1948, leaving only the tower. The best feature of its uncluttered interior is the late-19th-century stained-glass east window. Do not miss the three poignant and well-lettered tombstones in the churchyard, in memory of the three young daughters of William and Charlotte Pardington of nearby Armscote.

NORTHWICK PARK A-4 Situated in a great park on the slopes of the hills to the north of Blockley, this large 16th- and 17th-century mansion was built on the site of a vanished medieval village. It has an east front built in 1732 to the designs of the great advocate of Palladianism, Lord Burlington, and both mansion and outbuildings have now been extensively restored and converted into houses and flats. The nearby encampment, built during the 39-45 War, is now a business centre.

ODDINGTON B-6 Thinly spread on the lower slopes of the hill between Stow and the River Evenlode, and made up of Upper and Lower Oddington, this attractive village has several very pleasant houses including early-17th-century Oddington House, which was extensively remodelled in the early 19th century, and the nearby Old Rectory, which has had very much the same history. There are two excellent inns, the

The Horse and Groom, Upper Oddington

Fox in 'Lower' (*Tel: 01451 870 555*), and the Horse and Groom in 'Upper' (*Tel: 01451 830 584*). There is also an unassuming mid-19th-century 'new' church, but the village's best feature is some way off.

This is the old church of St Nicholas, which lies by itself at the end of a quiet road south of the village, although there is a long bridleway onwards from here to the village of Bledington. This remote church has had a number of illustrious owners, ranging from the Abbot of Gloucester to the Archbishop of York, and various kings of England, and it is known that Henry II stayed at Oddington several times. This distinguished ownership resulted in relatively ambitious building work in the 13th and 14th centuries, and thanks to its being largely unused in the 19th century, it has remained wonderfully unspoilt. See especially the Jacobean pulpit on its turned newel post, the lovely old chancel roof, the 15th-century font and Oddington's greatest treasure - its extensive and horrific late-14th-century 'Doom' wall painting. A few minutes' study of this fascinating relic of medieval times will show how easy it must have been for the clergy of the day to keep their primitive flock in a truly 'God-fearing' frame of mind.

Cottages on the green, Lower Oddington

Our **Walk 9** starts from Lower Oddington and passes Oddington's old church in its closing stages.

OXHILL C-3   A tidy, stone village in the 'Vale of Red Horse', with views south-eastwards to the scarp face of the Oxfordshire Cotswolds, where the Red Horse itself (see **Tysoe**) must have once been clearly visible, on its hilly slope above the straggling village of **Tysoe**. Oxhill has an attractively-signed, stone-built inn, the Peacock (*Tel: 01295 680 338*). There are also many pleasant farmhouses and cottages and the character of the village is not overawed by the modern building on its northern edge.

The interesting church has Norman north and south doorways, the south one being a much richer specimen than its counterpart. The tower is in the Perpendicular style and there is a fine 15th-century roof to the nave and a fascinating Norman font, ornamented with the rather scrawny figures of Adam and Eve at the Tree of Life. See also the fine 15th-century rood screen across the tower arch, and, in the south-eastern part of the churchyard, the grave of a female negro slave. She died in 1705, 'the property of 'Thomas Beauchamp, gent of Nevis', who was probably the owner of a sugar plantation, and who was almost certainly the husband of one of the local rector's twin daughters. This has little to do with Oxhill, but Nevis was the island in the West Indies where Horatio Nelson was to marry the widow Nisbet some eighty years later.

Our **Walk 14** starts from Oxhill.

PAXFORD A-4   This hamlet has few special features apart from the Churchill Arms (*Tel: 01386 594 000*), an inn with rooms, which also has a widespread reputation for good food. Unusually, being so close to the Cotswolds, there is still a brickworks here, just outside the village and close to the nearby railway line.

Our **Walk 3** starts from Paxford.

82

PILLERTON HERSEY C-2   This is centred upon a minute green with neatly-tended flowers around the base of its simple war memorial. There is a large modern house nearby overlooking a tree-shaded pool. Tucked away on the north side of the village there is a large Georgian rectory faced with mellow brick looking across the road to a pleasing church. This has a stout Perpendicular-period tower and an exceptional 13th-century chancel which is visible through a chancel arch distorted over the centuries into an almost horseshoe shape. Light floods into the interior through plain glass, some of which is of considerable age and of a slightly green hue. There are fine old roofs and interesting wood furnishings, much of the latter having been lovingly crafted by a Miss Mills, onetime lady of the nearby manor house. See also the

delightful little priest's doorway in the outer south wall of the chancel, the little stained-glass feature hanging in the window of the south-aisle chapel inscribed with the words *THINKE AND THANKE GOD. 1574,* and the handsome wall monuments in the west porch beneath the tower. Before leaving the churchyard do look at the amusing inscription on the tombstone of William Allibone close to the path from the west door.   Pillerton Hersey is on our **Walks 14** and **20**.

Pillerton Hersey Church

PILLERTON PRIORS C-2   In medieval times there was a grange here belonging to the Priors of Ware in Hertfordshire, hence this village's name. Little remains of any ancient houses here and the A422 dominates much of the village. However there is a track off this road leading southwards to the site of the church of St Mary Magdalene. Sadly this was burnt down in 1666, by coincidence the same year as the Great Fire of London. Although there is still a graveyard here, it is not known where the church was sited within it. The mystery remains but it is pleasant to linger here for a few minutes at least.

Pillerton Priors is on our **Walks 14** and **20**.

PRESTON-ON-STOUR A-2   Delightful village, with views over the willow-bordered Stour to Alscot Park, and although less than a mile from the busy A3400, it has an air of tranquillity that is hard to credit. There are two large timber-framed houses, the vicarage, and the Old Manor, and several smaller ones - a handsome Georgian house and several 19th-century neo-Tudor estate cottages. All these are close to sloping tree-shaded greens and above them stands Preston's interesting church. This has a medieval tower and nave which were carefully remodelled in the Gothick manner by the Chipping Campden architect, builder and quarry-owner, Edward Woodward, for James West of Alscot Park, who was much taken by this mode. The resulting 18th-century interior is a most stylish piece of work and contains an interesting series of monuments largely to members of the West family, notably those by Sir Richard Westmacott and by his eldest son, Richard. Do not overlook the beautiful classical sarcophagus in memory of Thomas Steavens, designed by James `Athenian' Stuart and sculpted by Thomas Scheemakers, nor, in contrast, the 17th-century monument to Sir Nicholas Kemp, with his two wives on either side. There is also a balcony and a fine 20th-century crucifix in memory of Sir Michael West. Don't miss the excellent copy of Hereford Cathedral's Mappa Mundi in the porch below the west tower.

Preston is on our **Walk 6**.

QUINTON, UPPER & LOWER A-3 There is a large housing estate here, but most of Lower Quinton remains unspoilt, with a village green overlooked by several thatched, timber-framed cottages, a handsome mellow-brick 17th-century house with Cotswold stone tiles, and a lively inn, the College Arms (*Tel: 01789 720 342*). This displays the arms of Magdalen College, Oxford, which still owns much land in the area. All this is overlooked by the splendid 130ft-high spire of Quinton Church. This has Norman south arcading and a Norman font, and many interesting features from the centuries that followed, including a Perpendicular-period clerestory, and an effigy of a knight who fought at Agincourt, Sir William Clopton, and a fine brass of his widow, Lady Clopton. On Sir William's death, this lady took a vow of widowhood, and is believed to have lived as an anchoress, or hermit, in a cell nearby. It is probably to her that we are indebted for the clerestory and the splendid spire.

It is possible to walk across the fields to Upper Quinton, where there is an early timber-framed manor house with very close vertical timbers. To the south of Upper Quinton is Meon Hill, one of the northern outliers of the Cotswolds. There are memories here of murder and suspected witchcraft in comparatively recent times, and the hill's summit is crowned by the ramparts of an Iron Age settlement.

RADWAY D-2 Delightful Hornton stone village beneath the partly-wooded slopes of **Edge Hill**. Many of its houses and cottages are thatched and at the far, southern end of the village there is a small green enriched by a tree-shaded pool and overlooked by further cottages and a little 19th-century chapel. The small spired church was built on a new site in 1866, to replace a brick building at the other end of the village. Its contents are not of great interest, apart from

Radway's parkland below Edge Hill

a monument brought here from the old church. This is to Captain Kingswell, a Royalist officer killed at the nearby Battle of Edgehill. There is also a plain wall monument to Sanderson Miller, who died in 1780 and to whom we refer below.

Sanderson Miller was squire of Radway and owner of Radway Grange, the handsome stone building in its own park, not far from the church. He was an outstanding 'gentleman architect', and one of the pioneers of the Gothick style, being at least three years ahead of the better-known Horace Walpole, who was soon to begin his own famous improvements to Strawberry Hill. Miller was responsible for a fascinating series of architectural works, from Wiltshire to East Anglia, including the Shire Hall at Warwick and Hagley Hall in Worcestershire. He made considerable alterations to his own home, the Elizabethan Radway Grange, and built the Edgehill Tower on the ridge above his park. This was intended to mark the spot where the Royal Standard was raised at the Battle of Edgehill. He also planted the hanging woods above the park and commissioned a large statue of Caractacus, which now stands in the garden of the Grange. This was originally intended for the Edgehill Tower, but was then found to be too large for its niche.

Radway Grange was, in Sanderson Miller's time, a centre of fashion and intellect, and Henry Fielding read the manuscript of his *Tom Jones* to Miller and his friends, Lord North, the Earl of Chatham and Sir George Lyttleton in its dining room. It is sad to relate that Miller spent the last years of his life in the house of a Lincolnshire doctor who specialised in the treatment of insanity. Read more about Sanderson Miller in Jennifer Meir's fascinating book, *Sanderson Miller and His Landscapes.*

Radway is on our **Walk 1**.

ROLLRIGHT STONES C-5 These consist of three separate features. First, *The King's Men* consisting of a Bronze Age stone circle about a hundred feet in diameter, and dating from between 2000 and 1800 BC. This group is situated to the immediate south of a minor road between the A3400 and the A44. Secondly, *The Whispering Knights*, the remains of a Bronze Age burial chamber, which stand four hundred yards to the east of the circle, and finally, *The King Stone*, an isolated 'standing stone', nearly opposite *The King's Men*,

The King's Men - Rollright Stone Circle

and almost certainly associated with them, although its exact purpose remains a mystery. These three features all lie in fine upland country, and there are splendid views, especially northwards from *The King Stone*. The ridge on which these stones stand is believed to have carried one of Britain's earliest and most important tracks - the so-called Jurassic Way, leading south and west along the limestone belt from the shores of the Humber, to Salisbury Plain and the coast beyond. For further reading on the subject of trackways in this area, see G.R.Crosher's *book, Along the Cotswold Ways.*

The 18th-century antiquary, William Stukeley, referred to the Rollright Stones as being '*corroded like worm-eaten wood by the harsh jaws of time*', but despite their exposed upland setting they still survive. In earlier times they were the subject of a legend relating to a king intent on the conquest of England, who was confronted here by a witch who spoke thus:

If Long Compton thou canst see,

King of England thou shalt be.

Unfortunately for the king and his followers this proved to be impossible at the time, and the witch continued :

As Long Compton thou canst not see

King of England thou shalt not be.

Rise up stick, and stand still, stone,

For King of England thou shalt be none.

Thou and thy men hoar stones shalt be,

And I shall be an eldern tree.

And so, it is sad to relate, the king, his men and his knights were all turned into stone, and the witch into an elder tree.

SALFORD C-6 This village just off the busy A3400 has no special features apart from its church. This was largely rebuilt by the very competent Victorian architect, G.E. Street, although it is not one of his better works. However, there is the base of an old cross in the churchyard, an interesting Norman font with interlaced arcading, and a crudely carved tympanum over the north doorway which may represent 'Sagittarius the Archer'. This subject was quite a favourite in the area - see also **Hook Norton**. There is a small inn here, the Black Horse (*Tel: 01608 642 824*). Walk from here to **Chipping Norton** or **Little Rollright** using **Shakespeare's Way**. There is also an inn at the cross roads, where the A44 is joined by the A436, just over a mile to the north-west of the village. Previously known as the Cross Hands, this is now called the Greedy Goose *(Tel: 01608 646 551)*. Our **Walk 17** starts from this inn.

SEZINCOTE A-5 In medieval times there was a small village here, but its church was destroyed by Cromwell's forces, due apparently to the estate being in the hands of an ardent Royalist family. In 1795 Sezincote was purchased by Colonel John Cockerell, a 'nabob' recently returned from Bengal. He died only three years later, leaving the estate to his younger brother Charles, who had served with him in the East India Company. Charles, who became a Baronet in 1809, and a Member of Parliament for Evesham, built a new house,

Sezincote - a distant view from the course of our Walk 18

employing another brother, Samuel Pepys Cockerell as his architect (he was distantly related to the diarist, Samuel Pepys).

S.P.Cockerell, who had already designed nearby **Daylesford** for Warren Hastings, was also Surveyor to the East India Company. He worked closely with Thomas Daniel, an artist who had also recently returned from India, and together they created a magnificent house in the Indian manner. This was at least in part inspired by the extensive works of the 16th-century Mogul Emperor, Akbar, who had deliberately mixed Islamic and Hindu styles in an attempt to integrate the diverse cultures of the two races. The result achieved at Sezincote is unique - a grand house in the authentic Mogul style in a rural English setting, the beauty of which was further enhanced by the outstanding landscape artist, Humphry Repton, who helped to create the lovely water gardens and lakes on the gently-sloping hillside that gives birth to the River Evenlode. In addition Sezincote offers a most elegant classical interior, which was beautifully restored in the mid-20th century. A visit here should certainly not be missed. *Details on www.sezincote.co.uk*

Sezincote was visited in 1806 by the Prince Regent who was staying with the Marquess of Hertford at Ragley, near Alcester, at the time, and it is thought that he was so impressed by Sezincote's style that he advanced his plans for the 'Indianisation' of his Pavilion at Brighton. Sadly the commission was given to the Prince's favourite architect, John Nash, rather than to Cockerell, but Sezincote must surely have been the Prince's inspiration.

For a delightfully nostalgic account of Colonel and Mrs Dugdale's frequent house-party weekends at Sezincote in the early 1930s, read John Betjeman's long poem, *Summoned by Bells*. This is extensively quoted in James Lees-Milne's highly informative book, *Some Cotswold Country Houses*. Our **Walk 18** passes close to Sezincote.

SHAKESPEARE'S WAY

A 146-mile long-distance footpath between Stratford-upon-Avon and the Globe Theatre, London, following as closely as possible the route that Shakespeare must have trodden on his many journeys between his Stratford home and London. It enters the area covered by this book at **Clifford Chambers** just to the south of Stratford-upon-Avon and leaves it just beyond **Chipping Norton**. It follows the

Shakespeare's Way, approaching Cherington

Stour Valley southwards as far as **Cherington** and then heads for **Long Compton** and **Little Rollright**. Similarly to the **Macmillan Way** it provides a fine opportunity to walk across Shipston Country and its other aim is to raise funds for Stratford-upon-Avon's Shakespeare Hospice.

For further information see www.shakespearesway.org See also - **Whichford Wood**, which is traversed by both of these long-distance paths.

SHENINGTON D-3 Standing over five hundred feet above sea level, Shenington is a stone and thatch village grouped around a large and attractive green and looks across the valley of the little Sor Brook to the smaller village of **Alkerton**. It has a welcoming inn, the Bell (*Tel: 01295 670 274*), which is noted for its imaginative meals and also offers rooms. Its church has a Perpendicular-period tower and porch, but it is otherwise largely in the decorated style. This was the result of heavy restoration in the 19th century by J.L.Pearson, best known as the architect of far-off Truro Cathedral. Our **Walks 13** and **15** both start from Shenington.

SHIPSTON-ON-STOUR B-4
'Sheepstown', as its name implies, was once an extremely important market for sheep, and its many delightful houses from the 17th, 18th and 19th centuries bear witness to a prosperity lasting for at least three hundred years. That it continued to thrive in the 19th century must have been due in part to the enterprise of the local canal and railway promoter William James of Henley-in-Arden, who in 1826 completed a tramway linking the canal wharfs of Stratford-

Shipston's colourful High Street

87

upon-Avon with Moreton-in-Marsh, with a branch line to Shipston opening some ten years later (*see* **Stratford and Moreton Tramway**). Eventually, in 1889, many years after Brunel's main Oxford, Worcester and Wolverhampton line came through **Moreton-in-Marsh**, part of the tramway was converted into a railway branch line between there and Shipston. Another factor contributing to Shipston's continuing prosperity was its position astride a busy north-south coaching route, and a number of its old

Shipston's mellow-brick bridge over the River Stour

coaching inns survive to this day, amongst them those in the very pleasant High Street, Shipston's little market square, including the George Hotel (*Tel: 01608 661 453*), and the White Bear *(Tel: 01608 661 588)*. These are just far enough away to escape the busy traffic of the A3400, Stratford to Oxford road. See also the Falcon Inn *(Tel: 01608 664 670)* and the Horseshoe Inn *(01608 662 190)* *both* in Church Street, and the Coach and Horses *(Tel: 01608 661 336)* which serves Hook Norton Ales.

St Edmund's Church has retained its 15th-century west tower, but is otherwise the creation of Victorian architect, G.E.Street. The interior is not of outstanding interest, but do not miss the very unusual conversion of a sounding-board from an earlier pulpit into an octagonal table. There is also a handsome little monument to another person to whom Shipston must have owed some of its prosperity, John Hart, who died in 1747 - *'A considerable Improver and Promoter of Manufacture in this his native Town'.* But of equal importance are Shipston's wealth of small- and medium-size shops, all of which offer helpful and friendly service in the tradition of a true market town. Shopping here is still a pleasure rather than a chore - long may it continue to be so. Our **Walk 19** starts from Shipston-on-Stour.

SIBFORD FERRIS and SIBFORD GOWER D-4 These two villages together with Burdrop, a minute hamlet sandwiched between them, form a large, widespread village. Ferris and Gower stand opposite each other on slopes above a quiet valley. Ferris has a large Quaker boarding school including one or two elegant 18th-century houses, and there is a short unfenced road from here with fine views, leading southwards past Woodway Farm. Gower has a wealth of Hornton stone and thatched cottages and a largely unremarkable Victorian church. However this is still worth visiting on account of the charming little monument to Mrs Isabelle Stevens (1907) by her son, Frank Lascelles, the once-renowned pageant master, who lived at the manor house.   The nearby Wykham Arms at Gower (*Tel: 01295 788 808*) stands at the start of our **Walk 12**, which first heads westwards across a valley to an old green road on its ridge, **Ditchedge Lane**.

STOURTON C-4 This small village lies just to the east of **Cherington**, of which it is now almost a part. Like Cherington, it has a number of pleasant houses and cottages, but it has no church or inn.

STOW-ON-THE-WOLD A-6   This attractive little market town is the focal point of the northern Cotswolds, with no fewer than eight roads converging upon its windy site, 700 feet above sea level. There was an Iron Age settlement here - an area of about thirty acres enclosed by earthworks, the partial remains of which are visible in Camp Gardens (but not, in our opinion, worth searching for). Some time later there was also a Roman villa, sited not far to the west of the **Foss Way**, which itself still runs along the western edge of the town.

The best of Stow is centred upon its large Market Square, and a weekly market and two annual fairs, known as the Charter Fairs, have been held here since 1107, when Henry I granted Borough status to 'Edwardstow', as it was then called. The connection of Stow-on-the-Wold with 'St Edward' remains a mystery as there are three possible candidates to be considered - Edward the Hermit, a shadowy figure from early Christian times, Edward, King and Martyr, the young king stabbed

The Market Square, Stow-on-the-Wold

to death at Corfe Castle, and the better-known King Edward the Confessor. We prefer the earliest candidate, Edward the Hermit, and we like to feel that this old bewhiskered saint spent his days in zealous prayer near the well that still bears his name below nearby **Maugersbury**.

Stow's fairs were renowned for the sale of wool and sheep, and Daniel Defoe, who once visited one of them, noted that over 20,000 sheep were then sold. However, since Defoe's time they have become better known for the sale of horses, and the Stow Horse Fairs are still held here in fields just to the west of the town. These take place twice a year, once in May and once in October.

Although undisturbed by any of the main roads entering the town, the Market Square is still usually busy with visitors and local country shoppers. There are several antique shops, picture galleries, hotels, restaurants and inns - all facing into the Square - and most are traditional 17th- or 18th-century Cotswold buildings, apart from handsome St Edward's House, faced with its Corinthian pilasters. There is a medieval cross here, although this has a headstone made in 1878, the year that St Edward's Hall was built a little to its north. This substantial Perpendicular-style building tends to divide the Market Square into two separate areas. It now houses the town's library. Beyond St Edward's Hall, the northern and more open half of the Square, known as `The Green', has wide grass verges and the old town stocks which were once used for the punishment of evil-doers. St Edward's Church lies well back from the Square, between this and the Foss Way. It is a large building with medieval origins, but much restored in the 17th century, following extensive damage caused while being used to house prisoners during the Civil War. The last battle in this bitter struggle between king and Parliament was fought at nearby **Donnington**, although it is usually referred to as the Battle of Stow. The church's interior was again restored in the 19th century, when the roof was rebuilt. The work was carried out by J.L.Pearson, the architect best known for the building of Truro Cathedral, but Stow's restoration does not appear to have been one of his better efforts. However, do not miss the impressive painting of the Crucifixion in the south aisle, thought to be by the 17th-century Flemish artist, Gaspar de Craeyer, nor the floor slab in memory of Francis Keyte, one of the Keytes of **Ebrington**, who was killed at the Battle of Stow.

Stow-on-the-Wold's church tower

Before leaving Stow, explore the small streets leading from the southern end of the Square where there are further shops and hotels, all contributing to Stow-on-the-Wold's qualities as an excellent touring centre for the northern Cotswolds. They include the bright little shopping precinct of Talbot Court. The town's excellent Tourist Information Centre *(Tel: 01452 831 082)* will be found at Hollis House, just off the Market Square.

Amongst the town's many hotels and inns are The Royalist *(Tel: 01451 830 670)*, The Unicorn *(Tel: 01451 830 257)*, The Grapevine *(Tel: 01451 830 344)*, The King's Arms *(Tel: 01451 830 364)*, The Old Stocks *(Tel: 01451 830 344)*, The Eagle and Child *(Tel: 01451 830 670)*, The Talbot *(Tel: 01451 870 934)* and The Queen's Head Inn *(Tel: 01451 830 563)*, which serves locally brewed Donnington ales.

THE STRATFORD AND MORETON TRAMWAY This was the brainchild of William James of Henley-in-Arden, near Stratford-upon-Avon, and was part of an ambitious scheme to link his other transport and mining interests to London, by a projected line entitled the Central Junction Railway. However, James was able to gain local support only for a line as far as Moreton-in-Marsh with a later branch to Shipston-on-Stour. An Act of Incorporation for this scheme was passed on 18 May 1821, just six weeks earlier than the Act of Incorporation for that of the world-pioneer line, the famous Stockton and Darlington Railway. It is interesting to speculate on what would have happened to Shipston-on-Stour and Moreton-in-Marsh if James's scheme for the Central Junction had been accepted in full. As it was, the local scheme soon ran into difficulties, both with problems of civil engineering, and with the prevention by the authorities of the use of steam trains on at least the first six miles south of Stratford-upon-Avon. The line to Moreton was finally opened in 1826, but by then James had been declared bankrupt, and all passenger and goods traffic was restricted to horse-drawn wagons provided not by the company but by toll-paying local traders.

In 1836 a branch line was opened to Shipston-on-Stour, and when Brunel's main Oxford, Worcester and Wolverhampton Railway line was built in 1853, the tramway provided a useful link to it at Moreton-in-Marsh. The Moreton-Shipston section was eventually converted to take steam trains, as a branch of the Great Western Railway, an arrangement that lasted until its final closure in 1960. The most enduring monument to the tramway is its mellow brick bridge over the Avon at Stratford-upon-Avon. The line of the tramway may be followed in several places, especially beside the Shipston Road out of Stratford, but its total disappearance in others is a reflection of the problems often facing archaeologists looking for signs of civilisation many hundreds or even thousands of years older. Read the most interesting story of this tramway in John Norris's book, *The Stratford and Moreton Tramway*.

STRETTON-ON-FOSSE B-4   An unspoilt village on a small hill just to the west of the busy **Foss Way**. The 'e' added to the word 'Foss' in the village's name is evidence of continuing confusion over the correct spelling of one of Britain's best-known Roman roads (see **Foss Way**). The church here was entirely rebuilt in 1841, and is not of great interest to visitors, but the William and Mary period Old Rectory and the Georgian Court House add some interest to the village. From a distance, the mellow and unusually restrained 19th-century manor house could easily be mistaken for a building some 300 years older. It overlooks the Foss Way, which crosses the line of the old **Stratford and Moreton Tramway** in the valley below. This was once the site of a small railway station, and the mellow-brick building that still stands here was once the Golden Cross Inn. This has been a private house for many years, but there is still an inn in the village - The Plough (*Tel: 01608 661053*).

SUNRISING HILL D-3 Steep sloping hill above the Vale of Red Horse (**see Tysoe**). For the outstanding view shown on our front cover take the path leading southwards from the A422 near the top of the hill, following **Macmillan Way** waymarks. There is a useful layby a few yards beyond the top of the hill.

SUTTON-UNDER BRAILES C-4 This village's wide green was once sheltered by a series of lofty elms, but sadly they all fell victims to the ravages of Dutch elm disease in the

On the Macmillan Way, just south of Sunrising Hill

1970s. The church has a well-proportioned south tower and the remains of an early Norman north doorway but the rather austere interior was not improved by restoration in the 1870s. Our **Walk 16** passes through Sutton-under-Brailes.

TALTON B-2   A quiet hamlet with a substantial house standing in gardens sloping down to the Stour and at nearby Talton Mill there is a very helpful farm shop.

TIDMINGTON C-4   Here is a 17th-century bridge over the River Stour, crossed by the ever-busy A3400, and overlooked by an old watermill. Well to the north, beside the garden of Tidmington House, a largely 17th-century building with a handsome 18th-century front, is one of Warwickshire's smallest churches. This has a late 12th-century tower with pyramid roof, and a 16th-century chancel; the rest having been rebuilt in about 1875. However, the early Norman font has an interesting carving of Christ upon it, and makes a visit here well worthwhile.

TODENHAM B-4   An attractive and unspoilt village, with views out across quiet countryside to the low wooded hills around **Cherington** and **Stourton**. It has a handsome late-Georgian manor house, and next to the church, a little mellow-brick 18th-century inn, the Farrier's Arms (*Tel: 01608*

Tidmington Church

650 901). The church of St Thomas of Canterbury dates largely from the 14th century and has a fine tower and octagonal, broached spire. There are many pleasing features in the Decorated-style here, including the east window, the sedilia, and the little priest's door on the south side. On the north side of the chancel will be found Perpendicular-style windows, which were added by the Greville family when they built a north chapel and north aisle in the early 16th century. Victorian restoration was carried out here with a very much lighter hand than at neighbouring **Lower Lemington**, and the interior of Todenham church is well worth a visit. See especially the 13th-century font with the names of the churchwardens of 1773 inscribed upon it, the brass to William Molton and his wife (1614), and outside, a memorial tablet on the south wall complete with skull and crossed bones.

TRAITORS' FORD D-4 Attractive ford in a deep valley with woodland on both sides of the road. This is known as Traitors' Ford, but the origins of its name are shrouded

in mystery - some think that a traitor was killed here, others believe that it was once known as *Traders' Ford*, the traders using it during their journeys with pack animals along **Ditchedge Lane**. Walk northwards from here using this delightful green road, from which there are fine views both to east and west. Traitors' Ford is on the course of the **Macmillan Way**.

TREDINGTON B-3 A very trim village in the valley of the Stour, with wide, well-mown grass verges and several interesting

Traitors' Ford

old houses. The village's White Lion Inn (*Tel: 01608 661 522*) stands on the main A3400 road and it is very pleasant to walk along the small road leading to the church of St Gregory, which is itself well worth visiting. It has a tall tower topped by a noble 15th-century spire - a landmark visible from many points of the delightful south Warwickshire countryside. It has a Norman south doorway and a Perpendicular-period two-storey north porch, beyond which will be found old stone floors, beautiful old benches, a handsome Jacobean pulpit, a Perpendicular rood screen, lovely roofs of the same period over nave and transepts, and also several interesting brasses. Architectural enthusiasts will note evidence of St Gregory's Anglo-Saxon origins, but everyone who comes here will sense an atmosphere of the past that lingers in this fine building.

TYSOE D-3 A long straggle of a village, comprising Lower, Middle and Upper Tysoe, all beneath the scarp face upon which the Red Horse was once carved (see below), and on the edge of wide valley country. This is known as the Vale of Red Horse and is intersected by a series of small streams flowing lazily north and west to join the River Stour. There is much modern development in this village but the little 'old fire station' with its thatched roof still stands next to the lively Peacock Inn (*Tel: 01295 680 338*), which ironically was itself largely destroyed by fire some years ago. The handsomely-pinnacled church has a Norman south doorway and a fine 14th-century font with sculptured figures of the Virgin and various saints. The interior is unfortunately rather cold in feeling, with walls scraped and pointed by over-enthusiastic Victorian 'restorers'. However do not miss the medieval and Jacobean seating nor the three interesting brasses.

Upper Tysoe is overlooked by a restored windmill, which unfortunately lost its sails some years ago (*see illustration on page 66*). It stands on a hill to the south of the village, part of the **Compton Wynyates** estate. For many generations this mill was worked by the Styles family of Tysoe and in the mid-nineteenth century there were no less than three windmills in the area, at Tysoe itself and also at Burton Dassett and Hornton, all of which were worked by three Styles brothers. Sadly the last miller Styles was killed during the 1914-18 war. For a wonderfully evocative account of life in Tysoe in the latter half of the 19th century and the early years of the 20th, read *Joseph Ashby of Tysoe* by his daughter, Miss M K Ashby. Joseph Ashby was much influenced in his youth by Joseph Arch, the founder of the National Union of Agricultural Workers, who lived at Barford near Warwick.

The great hill figure, the Red Horse, has long since disappeared, a victim of the enclosure of the village's open fields. It was originally cut into the red soil on the hillside above Tysoe, probably in medieval times. It was possibly cut on the instructions of Richard Neville, Earl of Warwick, known as The Kingmaker, in memory of the horse that he killed at the Battle of Towton, on Palm Sunday 1461, in an attempt to assure his wavering troops that he had no intention of retreating from the field. At first sight this seems an unlikely story, but it is interesting to note that the Red Horse was scoured for centuries at an annual ceremony on each Palm Sunday, the very anniversary of the battle where Neville killed his horse.

Tysoe is on our **Walk 15**.

UPTON HOUSE D-3 Given to the National Trust by the 2nd Viscount Bearsted, this fine William and Mary mansion is built of local Hornton stone and stands at the end of a straight driveway, off the main A422, Stratford-upon-Avon to Banbury road. It is situated less than

Upton House

*A quiet corner of
Upton House's garden*

half-a-mile behind the Edge Hill scarp, and from its south front there are pleasant views out over wide grassy terraces and beautiful, steep, sloping gardens, to its Temple Pool. This is enhanced by a little temple in the Tuscan style at its far end. This is said to have been designed by Sanderson Miller, squire of nearby **Radway**, and architect extraordinary. Miller may also have carried out improvements to the house in the 1730s, but upon this point there appears to be some doubt.

The interior of the present house is largely the work of the 20th-century architect, Morley Horder, who created a series of fine neo-Georgian rooms in about 1927. These provide a perfect setting for the remarkable collection of works of art presented by Lord Bearsted to the National Trust in 1948. This includes 18th-century furniture, Brussels tapestries, and 18th-century porcelain, both English and European. But of outstanding interest is the superb collection of pictures, with works by Bosch, the Brueghels, Holbein, Rembrandt, Van Dyck, Canaletto, Goya, El Greco, Tiepolo, Tintoretto, Constable, Hogarth, Reynolds, Romney and Stubbs. On no account should a visit here be missed, for it provides, in the heart of the English countryside, a sparkling insight into the rich diversity of European culture - an experience that many believe can only be achieved by visiting one of the world's great art capitals. However, visitors should not allow this wealth of art treasures to prevent them from seeing Upton House's extensive and very beautiful gardens. Time should be allowed for both. As with most National Trust properties there is also a good restaurant and a well-stocked shop (*Tel: 01295 670 266*).

WESTON PARK C-5 A pleasant, partly unfenced road runs through parkland between **Cherington** and **Long Compton**. This park once contained a fine early-19th-century mansion, but it was pulled down in 1934 and now only slight signs of a bare terrace remain. Read the fascinating story of Weston in *A Prospect of Weston in Warwickshire* by Michael Warriner, published by the Roundwood Press, but long out of print.

The Royal Oak, Whatcote

WHATCOTE C-3 A remarkably remote little village in the Vale of Red Horse - flat farming country between the Stour valley and the scarp face of the Oxfordshire Cotswolds. John Leland, the 16th-century antiquary, wrote of this area, `*Corn is the cheapest commodity grown in the county, whereof the Vale of Red Horse yieldeth abundantly*'.

Whatcote's church tower is in the Perpendicular style, but a Norman doorway and two windows are evidence of its much earlier origins. The south porch and part of the nave were damaged by a bomb on 12th December 1940 during the Second World War, but all has been made good and the interior is well worth visiting. See especially the three finely carved 15th-entury benches, the brass to William Auldyngton, and a fifteen-inch long, headless figure in mass vestments, dated 1511. There is a shaft of a medieval cross in the churchyard, this being crowned by an 18th-century sundial. See also the tablet in the church in memory of William Sanderson Miller, at one time rector of Whatcote. He was also the last Squire Miller of neighbouring **Radway** and a descendant of the 18th-century

Whichford Church

gentleman architect, Sanderson Miller (see **Radway**). There is a much-visited inn here, the warm and lively Royal Oak *(Tel 01295 680 319)*, which serves Hook Norton Ales.

WHICHFORD C-5 Here is a wide green overlooked by the attractive Norman Knight Inn *(Tel: 01608 684 621)* and surrounded by houses and cottages of almost every age - not outstandingly beautiful, but one of the most comfortable villages in the area. It is enfolded in beautifully-wooded hill country, not far from the Oxfordshire border, but well sheltered from the winds that blow around Great Rollright, on the hills to its south. The 18th-century rectory in mellow stone is one of the most elegant country buildings one could wish to encounter, and the church close by is equally attractive. This has a Norman south doorway, a rugged early-14th-century tower, and in contrast, a finely-built Perpendicular-period clerestory. The white-painted interior was restored in 1845, when neo-Gothic pews were installed, and these now blend in well with their surroundings. Do not miss the medieval stained glass in some of the window heads, nor the coffin lid, thought to be that of Sir John de Mohun, who

fought at the Battle of Boroughbridge in 1322, and who died shortly afterwards. See also the alabaster relief of John Merton, and the tomb chest with its brass of Nicholas Asheton, both men being rectors of Whichford in the 16th century.

Also visit the very interesting Whichford Pottery. For details see www.whichfordpottery.com or *(Tel: 01608 684 416)*.

Our **Walk 11** starts from Whichford.

On Shakespeare's Way in Whichford Wood

WHICHFORD WOOD C-5 Extensive woodland traversed by our **Walk 11**. It also contains an interesting meeting of two long-distance paths. It is here that **Shakespeare's Way** joins the **Macmillan Way,** as they head southwards together for a mile or two beyond **Long Compton**. From this junction point it is possible to walk 134 miles north-eastwards to Boston on the Lincolnshire coast, 153 miles south-west to Abbotsbury on the Dorset coast, a mere 21 miles northwards to Stratford-upon-Avon, or 125 miles south-eastwards to Shakespeare's Globe Theatre, on the banks of the Thames in London. This may all sound rather exhausting but, take heart, both paths have been walked in their entirety by people in their late seventies.

WHITCHURCH B-2 Minute hamlet beside the Stour with an attractive little church with Norman origins, which is well worth visiting. The once popular novelist, Ursula Bloom,

Norman doorway, Whitchurch Church

grew up in Whitchurch as her father, the Reverend Harvey Bloom, was Rector here for many years. Ursula Bloom died only in 1984 and lived for some years at Stratford-upon-Avon, about which she wrote in her book, *Rosemary for Stratford-upon-Avon*.

WILLINGTON C-4 A hamlet on gentle slopes above the River Stour with no outstanding features. It lies on **Shakespeare's Way** and this can be followed southwards across farming country to **Cherington**.

Bridge over the Stour at Wimpstone

WIMPSTONE B-2 This hamlet has only one feature of real interest - its mellow-brick bridge over the reed-bordered River Stour.

WINDERTON D-4 Beautifully sited on the steep southern slopes of a hill, with views over the tree-lined fields of the Feldon countryside to the tower of Brailes church. Here are farmhouses and cottages, some thatched, and all on different levels. The handsome Victorian church, built in 1878 by a certain Canon Thoyts, stands above the village, and its slender spire is a well-known local landmark. It has a very grand apsidal chancel enriched with alternate bands of red and white stone, and lancet windows with deep-coloured glass. This is Victorian architecture at its best and should on no account be missed. Those not interested in architectural details will at the very least enjoy the splendid views from the churchyard.

96